Agile Leadership Toolkit

The Professional Scrum Series by Scrum.org

Visit **informit.com/scrumorg** for a complete list of available publications.

The **Professional Scrum Series** from Pearson Addison-Wesley and Scrum.org consists of a series of books that focus on helping individuals and organizations apply Scrum and agile leadership to improve the outcomes of customers and organizations. Approaching the challenge from different perspectives, each book provides deep insights into overcoming the obstacles that both teams and organizations face as they seek to reap the benefits of agility.

All Scrum.org proceeds from the series go to Year Up, an organization whose mission is to close the Opportunity Divide by providing urban young adults with the skills, experience, and support to empower them to reach their potential through professional careers and education.

Make sure to connect with us!
informit.com/socialconnect

Pearson Addison-Wesley

informIT.com
the trusted technology learning source

O'REILLY® Safari

Agile Leadership Toolkit

Learning to Thrive with Self-Managing Teams

Peter Koning

Addison-Wesley

Boston • Columbus • New York • San Francisco • Amsterdam • Cape Town
Dubai • London • Madrid • Milan • Munich • Paris • Montreal • Toronto • Delhi • Mexico City
São Paulo • Sydney • Hong Kong • Seoul • Singapore • Taipei • Tokyo

For information about buying this title in bulk quantities, or for special sales opportunities (which may include electronic versions; custom cover designs; and content particular to your business, training goals, marketing focus, or branding interests), please contact our corporate sales department at corpsales@pearsoned.com or (800) 382-3419.

For government sales inquiries, please contact governmentsales@pearsoned.com.

For questions about sales outside the U.S., please contact intlcs@pearson.com.

Visit us on the Web: informit.com/aw

Library of Congress Control Number: 2019944338

Cover illustration: SeamlessPatterns/Shutterstock; HappyPictures/Shutterstock

ISBN-13: 978-0-13-522496-0
ISBN-10: 0-13-522496-9

1 2019

To my wife Marieke, my buddy and best friend.

Contents

FOREWORD

We live in uncertain times created by the move from the age of mass production to the digital or software age. Traditional management and leadership practices were developed to manage work, to build the process, and to provide the intelligence for work to be done. Workers were cogs, resources to be applied along with other assets such as tools and capital to get work done. The management was the king, directing and leading the work. That is all changing. We are moving to a world where, by necessity, teams have to be empowered to respond to their environment. Agility is turning the world upside down with traditional hierarchical, Taylorism management, which is being replaced with something new. Agile leadership is the future. But what does an agile leader do?

There have been many books written about what agile leadership is. They describe the change to servant leadership, the role of organization, and even behaviors that we expect from these new leaders. But they do not provide you with tools you need to work as an agile leader. In this book, Peter has provided an integrated toolkit for agile leadership. He has provided a set of tools that ask the right questions, provide focus, raise transparency, and allow adaption. They can be thought of as a set of tools that provide a foundation for agile leadership. That does not mean that if you use the tools you will be "agile." The path to building the right environment for agility to thrive is a hard one. But this is a great place to start.

To thrive in the digital age requires a step change, not just in terms of the adoption of new technology, team practices, or process but also the environment those "things" are brought into. Leadership needs to change, and the framework that Peter describes not only provides practical tools but also focuses the leader on the right things. Ownership, time to learn, building the right habits, and setting the right goals are the fundamental elements for agility.

—Dave West

Dave West is the CEO and Product Owner at Scrum.org. He is a frequent keynote speaker at major industry conferences and is a widely published author of articles and research reports. He led the development of the Rational Unified Process (RUP) for IBM/Rational. After IBM/Rational, West returned to consulting and managed Ivar Jacobson Consulting for North America. Next, he served as VP and research director at Forrester, where he ran the software development and delivery practice. Prior to joining Scrum.org, he was Chief Product Officer at Tasktop where he was responsible for product management, engineering, and architecture.

PREFACE

A leader is like a farmer, who doesn't grow crops by pulling them but instead creates the perfect environment for the crops to grow and thrive.

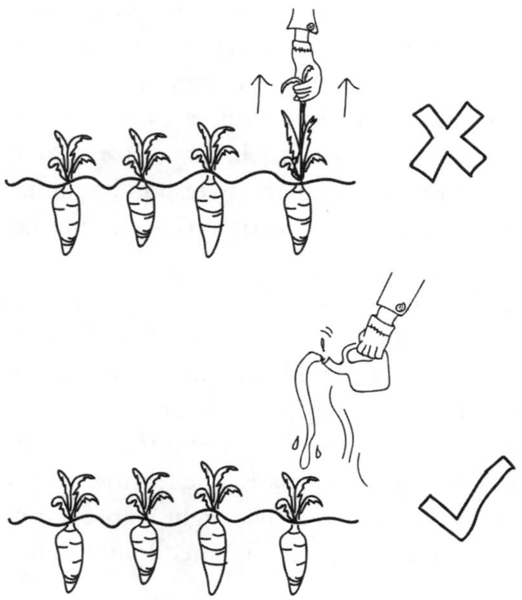

INTRODUCTION

How do you create this thriving environment for self-managing teams? How do you facilitate teams in such a way that they take real ownership? How do you create enough structure to prevent chaos but also avoid falling back into micromanagement? Is your role as a leader to sit on your hands and trust the autonomy of the teams? These and similar questions are ones I've been asked and also have asked myself for the past decade.

Take for example David, a manager of several software development teams. I coached David over a period of months, and together we discovered several tools. After testing these tools in other companies and situations, I repeatedly saw the proof that these tools really build this thriving environment for self-managing teams.

Let's go back a few years for an explanation of the situation David was in. He had been managing these teams for just over three months and was thinking about what he had to do next. The first weeks in his new role were fantastic. There was real energy and passion in the department. Most team members were interested in the new way of working and were happy that they could finally start working in an agile way as well. In order to beat the competitors and to become a market leader again, they needed to become more agile as a company. They needed to accelerate and get product improvements to the market faster. They recently had been overtaken by rivals who had been able to rapidly gain market share by responding quickly to new opportunities; they needed to change direction to regain market leadership.

David did not doubt his choice to become a manager. This new way of managing fit well with his passion. He really wanted to create an environment in which his teams could flourish, improve, innovate, and thrive—an environment of trust, inspiration, and focus on the customer. But he was missing the answers to a few important questions. We met at his company. I could see the pride and passion he felt toward his teams but also the doubt and struggle for the next step. The night before our meeting, as he lay awake, he wrote down the things that haunted him. His most important questions were

1. What are proper goals that focus on the customer instead of the internal organization?
2. How can my teams flourish and thrive in the long run?
3. Which metrics or signals are indicating that my teams are doing the right things?
4. What do I have to do to create a culture of continuous improvement?

He knew that analyzing the situation, drawing up plans, setting individual goals, and managing budgets were not the answer to his questions. His situation was far too complex for this analytical approach. The unpredictable markets, the customer expectations, and the dynamics in his teams were just too complex for a straightforward plan. He felt he needed a totally different approach. His million-dollar question to me was: *how do I create the right environment for my teams so they can thrive?* David explained that he didn't want to be the leader who always has to give the answer to these questions. He trusted his teams to answer these questions in a much better way. But how could he create an environment in which the answers to these questions could be explored and discovered? I promised to help him find these answers, even though back in those days, I didn't have the answers yet either. But together we tried, failed, learned, and improved.

This book is the result of a three-year search for these answers. The results are practical and concrete tools and examples for your specific situation. It gives you the ability to create an environment in which your teams focus on the goal, take ownership, learn quickly from the customers, and improve the culture.

Nobody wants to lead people who are unmotivated, deliver low-quality products, and do not collaborate with other teams, nor do they want to lead where highly talented people leave. Unfortunately, there are too many companies that struggle with at least a few of these bad things. Scrum, Less, and other agile methodologies promise motived, collaborative, and high-performing teams. In numerous cases I've seen these teams. They are truly empowering, energetic, and contagious, and customers are enthusiastic about the quality and speed of the improvements they make. But getting teams to this level of performance is not easy. Every team, department, product, and customer base is so unique that there is no recipe or "7 steps to success" to be found. But luckily, there are several practical tools that you can use to create the tailor-made environment for your teams and your customer base.

My passion is to share these tools with you so that you can create a working environment in which people like their jobs and grow as people in their skills and self-confidence.

AUDIENCE—WHO IS THIS BOOK FOR?

This book is intended for leaders in an agile environment. They have recently become or already are responsible for people in agile teams, for several agile teams, complete agile departments, or even agile companies. These leaders are already convinced of the benefits and necessity of agile and are searching for ways to improve. They are globally familiar with Scrum and other frameworks. In addition, they already have experience with managing teams in general, and now they are looking for practical tools, handy metrics, and new methods to create an inspiring environment for their self-managing teams. Last but not least, their company is active in a competitive market. This means customer satisfaction, innovation, digitization, and quality are king.

RESPONSIBILITY OF AN AGILE LEADER

Agile leaders lead their teams in a totally new way. They lead because they create precisely the environment that the teams need to grow and improve. Within this environment, the teams optimize the processes themselves, increase their own effectiveness and efficiency, and make all kinds of decisions on a daily basis. That makes these teams self-managing. They organize their own work and they have all the skills to do so. These agile teams are agile in and of themselves because they can respond quickly to new technologies, threats from competitors, and the ever-changing expectations of their customers. They don't have to wait for official approval, management decisions, or top-down strategic changes. Because they have a short feedback loop with their customers and users, they can continuously experiment with new ideas, improve their products and services, and align with other self-managing teams.

The agile leader is the architect of this environment—just as a farmer doesn't grow crops by pulling them but instead creates the perfect environment for the crops to grow and thrive. When the crops don't grow, he doesn't blame the crops; rather, he sees it as feedback on the environment he created. The same goes for an agile leader. He takes the humble responsibility to create this environment for his people and teams. When the teams don't flourish, when things go wrong, or when customers are not satisfied, the new leader doesn't punish his people for doing wrong things; he sees it as feedback of the environment he created. He asks for feedback and help from his employees to find improvement, and together they adapt and improve the environment.

Agile Leadership Toolkit

Agile leaders provide an inspiring environment for their agile teams to thrive. But how do they create such an engaging environment? This requires not only a new mindset but a lot of new skills, unlearning the old and learning the new ones. People learn not by only reading a book but by a lot of doing. Therefore, the tools in this book are very practical. Take, for example, a chef. He becomes a master cook because he spends hours and hours in the kitchen practicing with knives, pans, ingredients, and all kinds of other tools. The same goes for agile leaders. They become masters in leading inspiring environments because they practice a lot. To help agile leaders, this book provides practical tools, workshops, metrics, and examples to put immediately into practice. And by applying them, the underlying skills needed to become an agile leader can grow and develop.

The tools, workshops, metrics, and examples form a cohesive toolkit for the agile leader. The toolkit is the new steering wheel to redefine how today's organizations could be led. See Figure P.1 for the visualization of the toolkit.

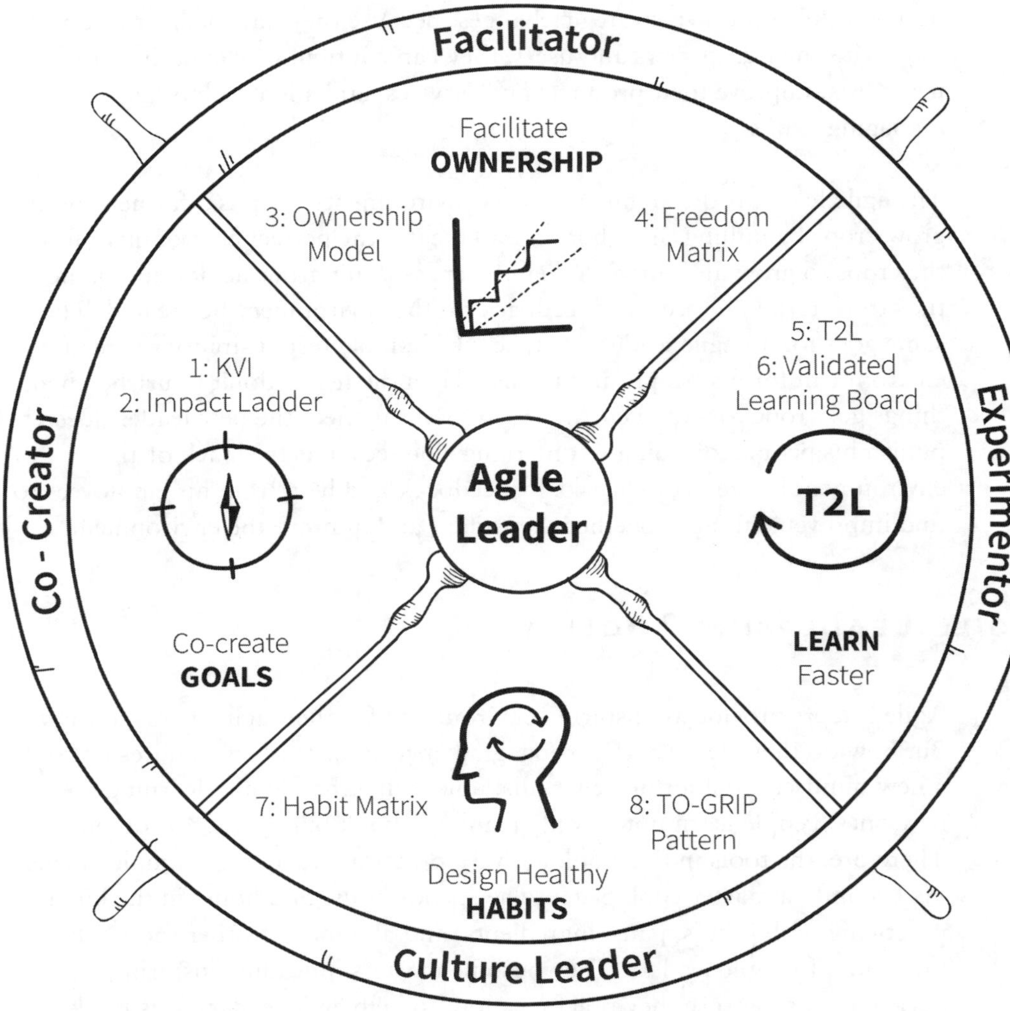

Figure P.1 The toolkit

The toolkit of the agile leader is divided into four parts, which together describe the environment that self-managing teams need to thrive. The agile leader has the following practical tasks:

1. Co-create goals
2. Facilitate ownership

3. Learn faster
4. Design healthy habits

Successful agile leaders provide their teams with the support they need by successfully mastering each of these four parts. They can make better decisions based on the clear goal, create perseverance and energy with ownership, and respond quickly based on fast learning ability, all in an inspiring culture with healthy habits. Each part of this toolkit is described in one section of the book. Each consists of two practical tools and a concrete skill of the agile leader—in total, eight tools and four skills. The skills are put into practice in the last section of each part, and they are explained in such a way that leaders can immediately start working with them. Each tool can be successfully used separately, but each tool reinforces the other tools in an additive way.

The eight toolkit tools are as follows:

1. **Key Value Indicator (KVI).** The KVI is for the teams and is the most important indication that they deliver value.
2. **Impact Ladder.** The Impact Ladder is used for brainstorming and visualizing the customer impact. This supports teams in continuously improving products and services to increase the benefit for the users.
3. **Ownership Model.** The Ownership Model visualizes what teams need to take ownership.
4. **Freedom Matrix.** The Freedom Matrix visualizes the freedoms and responsibilities of the team.
5. **Time to Learn (T2L).** T2L measures the speed of learning. It is a calculation of the time it takes from when it is built until the team learns from actual usage by customers.
6. **Validated Learning Board (VLB).** A VLB is used to visualize the learning flow of the team.
7. **Habit Matrix.** The Habit Matrix supports culture change and the designing of new habits.
8. **TO-GRIP.** This tool supports the agile leader in making big changes and improvements in the environment.

The four skills are as follows:

1. **Co-create.** The ability to co-create the vision and the direction in which to go. Together with the agile teams, the leader creates the focus on delivering value for the customers and company.
2. **Facilitate.** The ability to facilitate ownership not by enforcing it but by facilitating the process of continuously improving ownership.
3. **Experiment.** The ability to create a safe environment in which teams run experiments. This is not an environment in which teams are blamed for their mistakes but one in which the leader mentors the teams so they continuously learn from customers and improve.
4. **Lead the culture.** The ability to create a healthy culture and lead people not by telling them what to do but by leading the culture.

With this toolkit, agile leaders can create the desired environment, continuously improve, and make adjustments where necessary. Agile teams therefore have an inspiring goal, a great deal of ownership, a high learning speed, and a good culture. This is the ideal environment for teams to be successful. It makes them agile at high speed.

Why This Book?

Since 2015, I have actively looked for concrete tools that support the agile leaders in their responsibilities. My experience with Scrum taught me that tools help teams to become agile, and that the best way to improve is to start working in the new way. Agile leaders also need practical tools, metrics, and meetings to help them start working in a new way, and by doing so to become increasingly better agile leaders. Together with several different companies, in many different contexts, I've developed these tools into this toolkit. This book shares what I have learned.

READING GUIDE

Each part of this book can be read separately and used individually. The numerous examples are often based on my experiences at various companies with a wide variety of different managers and leaders, as well as my own experiences as a manager. Because not all examples are positive, I have chosen to anonymize them; any resemblance to a specific company or situation is purely coincidental. In addition, I use the masculine "he" to refer to the agile leader simply because it seems less awkward than "he or she." Obviously, this is not intended to make a statement about whether men or women are better agile leaders.

Because I wanted to write a very practical book with tools, step-by-step plans, and workshops, the titles of many sections are based on concrete questions that agile leaders have asked me in recent years. In order to make the book as self-contained as possible, there are only a few references in this book to external research or sources. The toolkit is also not partial to Scrum or any other particular agile framework; it can be used with any agile approach. The focus is on practical tips and tools, examples, and anecdotes that illustrate the toolkit. Extra examples and templates of the various tools in this book are available on www.tval.nl.

During the search for these tools, the image of a sailboat in uncharted waters helped me to find the tools and make them concrete. The ship has to sail over unknown and unpredictable waters, and the sailors want to get to their destination as quickly as possible. What makes them successful? They need a compass to navigate and check their bearings. They need a lot of wind to move and be faster. The sailboat must be agile at high speed, able to respond quickly when something happens, and capable of learning continuously. The crew prefer to sail through a beautiful environment. The first part of the toolkit, "Co-create Goals," inspires the target for the compass. Facilitating ownership provides the speed. The third part, "Learn Faster," improves the reaction speed and agility. And the culture and habits make it all a beautiful environment.

AFTER READING THIS BOOK

By reading this book and learning how to apply the described tools and tips, agile leaders are better able to shape the new organization. They

- have concrete tools and tips to improve the environment,
- know what self-managing teams need to thrive,
- have, themselves, grown in their role as agile leaders,
- know better what their role is at specific moments,
- are able to keep the hard side and soft side of continuous improvement in balance, and
- can really thrive when leading agile teams.

Register your copy of *Agile Leadership Toolkit* on the InformIT site for convenient access to updates and/or corrections as they become available. To start the registration process, go to informit.com/register and log in or create an account. Enter the product ISBN (9780135224960) and click Submit. Look on the Registered Products tab for an Access Bonus Content link next to this product, and follow that link to access any available bonus materials. If you would like to be notified of exclusive offers on new editions and updates, please check the box to receive email from us.

Acknowledgments

I want to thank many people for making this book possible, but it's impossible to list them all here. I especially want to thank my wife for always supporting me and giving me honest and candid feedback. I want to thank Prowareness for giving me an awesome job that allows me to write books. I want to thank all the people whose quotes appear at the start of each section.

I want to thank Scrum.org and Dave West for writing a preface and adding this book to the Professional Scrum Series. My thanks go also to Kurt Bittner for reviewing my book, improving the English, and especially brainstorming with me on the overall idea and theme of the book.

I also want to thank Selina Sandberg for making the awesome visuals and illustrations.

Last but not least, I want to thank the dozens of customers and clients over the decade who gave feedback, brainstormed, and asked hundreds of questions. Thanks to all of these people, I could experiment, try, fail, learn, improve, and discover all of these tools!

About the Author

Peter Koning has been responsible for many agile teams for many years. After studying computer science at the University of Leiden, he started as a programmer and team manager. In 2005, he took his first steps in the agile mindset and the Scrum framework, the first years as manager of teams in the Netherlands and Romania. Partly because of this, he learned the importance of a good culture. In the years that followed, he fulfilled various roles, such as Scrum Master, team manager, agile project manager, and department manager. As an agile project manager, he was responsible for a large project that involved a complete rebuild of the flagship of an organization. He has come to understand the importance of quickly learning from real users. As a department manager, he was responsible for various agile teams in both the run and change environments. That taught him the importance of ownership and facilitating the right environment in which the teams can take this ownership.

In recent years, he has worked at Prowareness as a senior leadership consultant and entrepreneur. He has advised, trained, and coached all kinds of managers in agile leadership. In addition, he supervised several agile transformations and gave a lot of training and workshops. Peter is also the entrepreneur of Relead, a company within the Prowareness family that focuses on training, mentoring, and advising leaders and leadership teams.

PART 1
Co-Create Goals

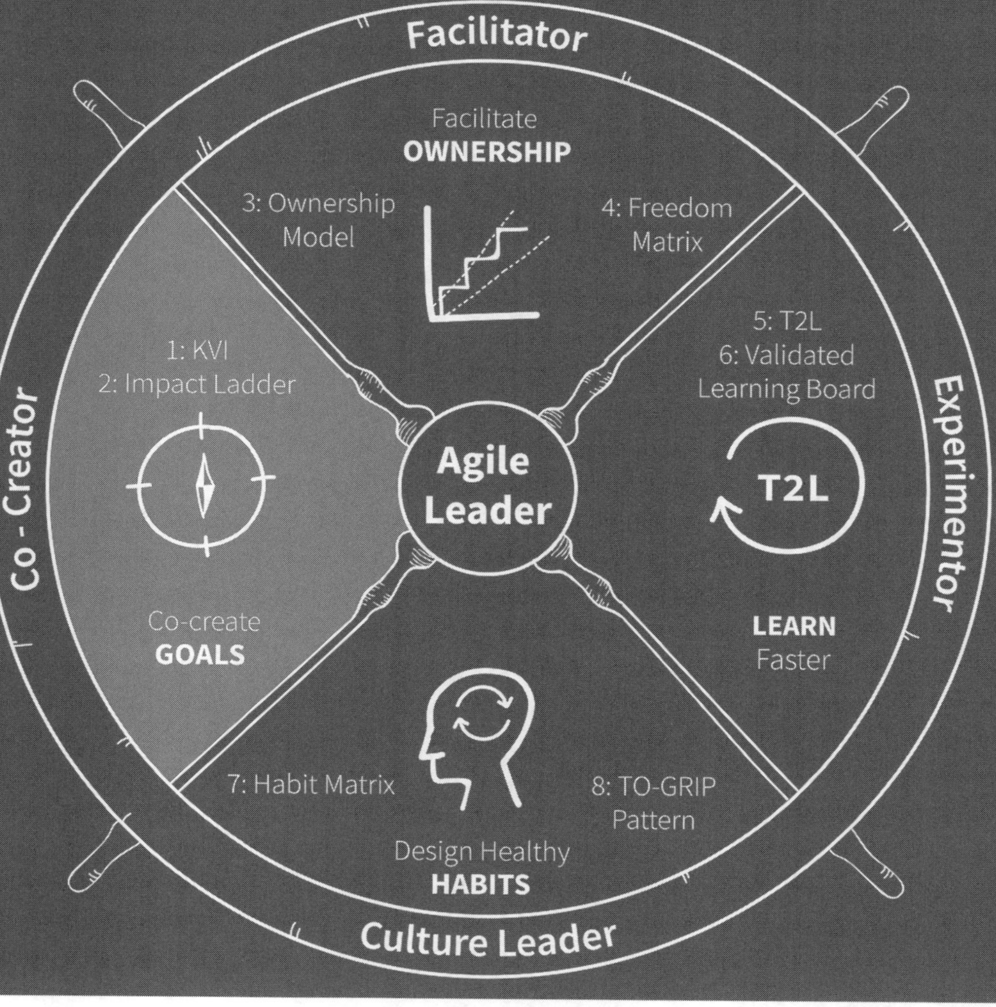

1.1 HOW DO YOU SET THE RIGHT GOALS?

Teams without clear goals will not achieve their goals clearly!

– Tom Gilb

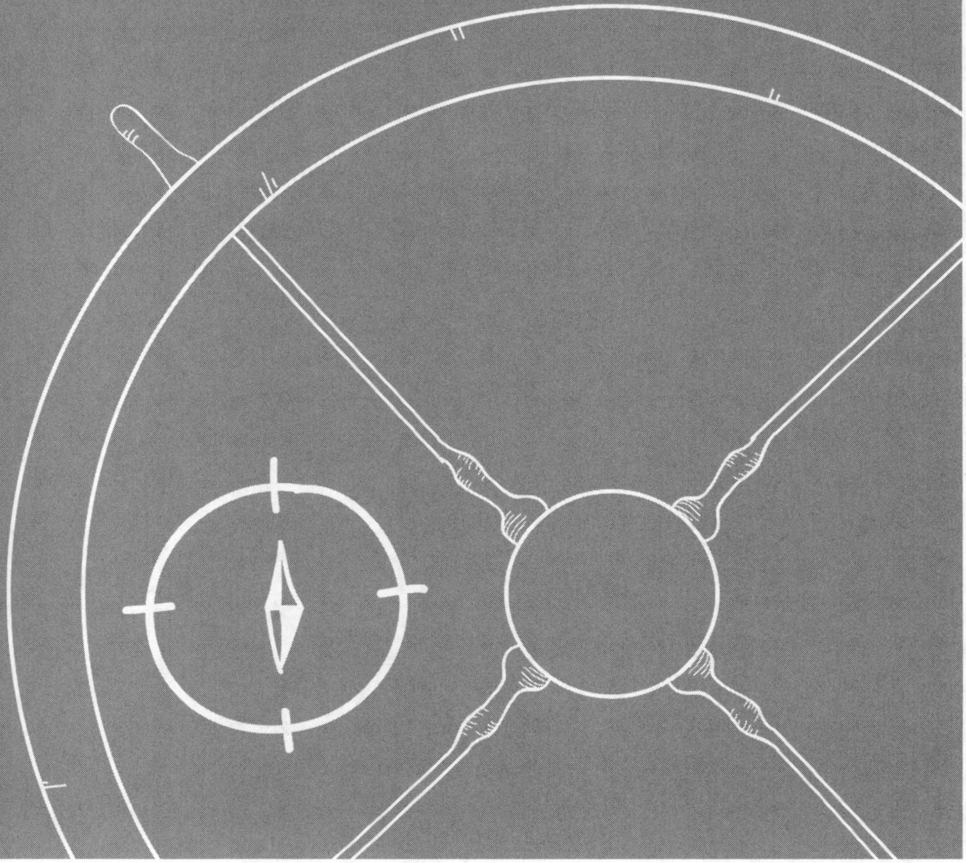

Introduction Questions

Co-create **GOALS**

1. What does "winning the match" mean for your teams?
2. What metric indicates that the teams are working smarter and are more successful?
3. Does this metric show that the customer impact has increased?

Introduction Story

It is early January. Director Phil is opening the new year in his company today. With a combination of humor, anecdotes, vulnerability, and passion, he is able to captivate the people. He tells what he expects from his people next year. The different objectives are concrete and measurable, and most of his colleagues have a clear understanding of them. The objectives involve at least 95% customer retention, a partner program for the top 10% of customers, and 20% growth from existing products and services. In addition, goals include 100% growth in the innovation turnover, close cooperation with partners, and the requirement that employees meet their monthly targets. For the latter, Phil has come up with a nice reward: everyone who gets his or her target can join the international *hackathon*—two days of innovation, experimenting, and learning from one another. The hackathon announcement is received with applause. Finally, Phil presents the five key performance indicators (KPIs) that are decisive for the bonus for the various departments. The objectives are specific, and it is clear what must be done. Most employees are looking forward to it.

After his presentation, there is a break with coffee and tea and a piece of cake with the logo of the company. Phil goes from group to group to ask employees for feedback on his story. He starts doubting whether the core of his message has arrived because everyone appears to have a different picture of what is most important this coming year. Phil wonders if they have listened. Was everyone still busy with the Christmas holidays or secretly on their phones? In the end, Phil concludes that it is up to him. Apparently, despite all his good intentions, he did not offer enough focus. He has mentioned many important things, but which main goal determines whether it will be a good year? When will the teams win the match? If they achieve all the objectives, is it guaranteed a successful year? Or just a lost year? Is it possible that everyone thinks they are doing well, but in the end it was not good enough?

Phil realizes that he has not done well. Just like in a sports competition, the score on the board is the most important thing. Everyone knows that. No player has to look at the board to know the score; they all already know. Phil understands that this score is not visible in his company and that he has not given any clarity in his story.

Phil decides to organize a brainstorming session with his leadership team (LT) for the same afternoon. After sharing his observations of that morning and assigning the blame to himself, he discusses the need for focus. The whole LT agrees on the urgency of focus. But what that focus should be is a whole different ballgame. Different goals seem important—turnover and profit but also innovation, customer satisfaction, and quality. In the end, they make a choice together. There is an all-important KPI for every team.

They decide to give it a nickname: the KVI—key value indicator. They have some ideas for this KVI, but they want to sketch them together with a few teams, using the ideas of the teams to make the objectives more concrete and inspiring. The goals must help the teams to really focus on the customer and deliver a positive customer impact. This KVI indicates for the teams whether they win the competition and whether they successfully create value for the customers and for the company.

Months later, Phil notes that the teams are now much better able to solve problems, implement improvements, and come up with initiatives on their own. In specific situations, they can better assess the advantages and disadvantages themselves and make choices without needing the approval or decision from the LT. This increases the agility and productivity of the teams. Phil finds it nice to see that they can now independently impact the customer and thereby increase the value for the company.

TRADITIONAL VERSUS NEW GOALS

Teams operate in a complex environment. Markets, technologies, competitors, and customers' wishes change so quickly and so unpredictably that teams need a new type of goal to give them direction. I'll explain why.

In static or slow-changing markets, the performance of employees and teams can be measured relatively easily by measuring what they *do*, on the output. An employee or team that produces more has a higher performance than others. So the more tires mounted, phone calls handled, or windows painted, the higher the performance. This is because, in these markets, there is a relatively stable correlation between what a company produces, the benefit for its customers, and the value for the company. Many companies have existing products that they want to sell to more customers. And the different departments in the organization have to produce more output with a certain customer satisfaction level and, preferably, lower costs. Setting goals for these departments and teams can be done by focusing on an internal metric, often called key performance indicators (KPIs). These metrics can be measured by just looking at the numbers of that specific department. Examples include the number of cars produced, phone calls made, first-time-right numbers, or software functionalities delivered. There is a stable and predictable correlation between what the teams do and what the company achieves.

But in complex, unpredictable, or fast-changing markets, this correlation is often unknown. It may be known today, with the current market situation, but change is almost a guarantee, and therefore this correlation could become unknown in the near future. Nokia was a successful phone company for many years. The organization got into a tough spot not because it didn't produce enough telephones or because we customers stopped using cell phones. One of the reasons for this tough spot is because the company couldn't pivot fast enough to smartphones.

If a sports team focuses fully on ball possession, this possession will increase. But more ball possession doesn't automatically mean winning the game. Likewise, more handled phone calls, more functionalities in the app, or more customer visits are no guarantee for success. Objectives that define what the team has to *do* don't make them more successful. Rather, objectives must indicate what the team must *achieve*. This means, for example, not the number of videos rented but the number of hours people watch videos—because thanks to new technologies, we rent fewer videos (in the shop) but we watch more videos than ever before.

The new way of setting goals is focused on what teams need to *achieve* and not anymore on what to *do*. These new goals make it tangible when defining what "winning the game" means. These goals therefore indicate when teams are really successful. Measurable goals that are based on what they have to *achieve* tend to be stable when the market changes. To put it in other words, agile leaders create an environment in which goals are clear, inspiring, and measurable on what has to be *achieved*; this gives a stable direction even though the solution is uncharted and yet unknown. The goals are also stable when new technologies emerge and new possibilities have to be embraced.

> *Agile leaders create an environment in which goals are clear, inspiring, and measurable on what has to be achieved; this gives a stable direction even though the solution is uncharted and yet unknown.*

So how can leaders give these types of goals to teams—that provide areas to focus on but also empower them to respond to market changes and new technologies? How can leaders use the collective thinking power of the team to continuously monitor, adapt, and improve while preventing the team from setting the wrong priorities, making the wrong choices, or having the wrong focus? How can leaders give their teams a compass to go in the right direction in uncharted waters?

There is a relatively simple solution to this challenge. In order for teams to measure their success, they have to know that they have to look outside the building. Stop looking at internal KPIs and start looking at the customers. Teams can measure their success by how much impact they have delivered to their customers. When they know that they have made their users more successful or satisfied, they know they are successful themselves. Next, they can use this insight to improve; they can brainstorm and run experiments on how to improve in the next period (more on this topic in Part 3, "Learn Faster"). It's crucial that the environment in which they work supports focusing on the customer and not on the internal output. A practical tool to change the environment is using a new type of metric. This metric expresses the relation between what the teams deliver, how this benefits the customer, and how that brings value to the company. This is why they need an indicator on the delivered value.

Tool 1: Key Value Indicator

The KVI is the most important indicator for the team to find out whether they generate value. The KVI is preferably one metric, visualized in a trend line, that makes the relationship between customer impact and value for the company tangible. The purpose of this tool is illustrated in Figure 1.1. Teams have to serve customers smarter and better; that generates more value for the company. It is therefore not an internal goal that measures what the team does. Instead, it's an externally focused goal that measures (directly or indirectly) the behavior of the customers. The KVI is a current figure with which the team can measure the consequences of their actions. Several teams that work on the same customer impact can have the same KVI.

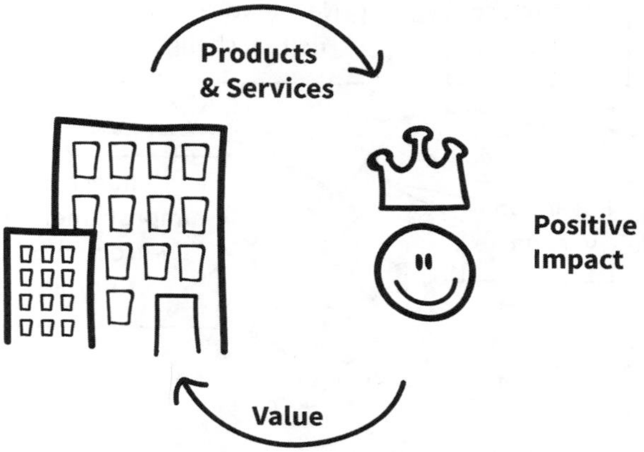

Figure 1.1 Visualization of the KVI

Many companies have been working with KPIs[1] or objectives and key results (OKRs)[2] for years. The power of these tools is that they give focus. They often measure the efficiency and quality of the internal process. But in a complex and dynamic market, it is important that teams focus on the customer. That is why the KVI is a customer-oriented tool that enhances the power of KPIs and OKRs. When KPIs and OKRs also measure the impact had on the customer, they are probably already KVIs. In other words, the most important KPI that also indicates the positive customer impact and how that brings value to the company is a KVI. Next, I give a few examples of KVIs. Other examples can be found at www.tval.nl.

1. https://kpi.org/KPI-Basics
2. https://rework.withgoogle.com/guides/set-goals-with-okrs/steps/introduction/

SOME EXAMPLES OF KVIS

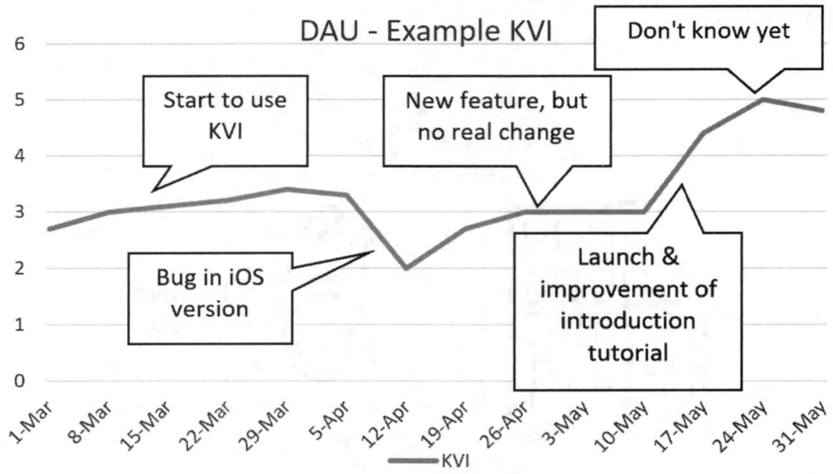

Figure 1.2 Example KVI

Some examples of KVIs include the following:

1. A team that develops an online sports game has, as a KVI, the daily active users (DAU): the number of (millions of) users who play every day. A large proportion of these users just use the game for free, and about 15% have a paid subscription. These more serious gamers bring in the revenue. The percentage has been very stable over the years; as the DAU rose, so did the monthly income. Therefore, the DAU is a proper indicator of delivering value both to the customers and to the company. People who really love the game play it daily. And the more people who play it daily, the higher the revenue.

   The DAU was known to everyone. When team members came in the morning, they asked each other about the DAU, and they followed how it developed over the course of the day. New functionalities, improvements, and marketing campaigns were measured in terms of increase (or decrease) of the DAU. New employees are updated on historical increases through good functionalities. Painful drops due to bugs, unsuccessful features, or not responding quickly enough to competitors are shared with a smile and a tear. In Figure 1.2, the rise and fall of the DAU is visualized. As illustrated, several events influenced the DAU.

2. A software company is searching for a proper KVI. It has many customers that use its product on a daily or weekly basis. The company used to track the net promotor score (NPS), but over the past months the employees noticed that their NPS wasn't giving them the insight they needed. Looking at the customers that filled in the NPS, they saw that a very low percentage took the time to give feedback but that most of the not-so-happy customers did take the time. Next they wanted to know the correlation between the amount of the monthly subscription and customer satisfaction. The monthly subscription varied between $10 and more than $5,000 per month. Together with some product managers, they brainstormed on this dilemma. They asked themselves two questions. How can the KVI give insight on the following?

   - The satisfaction of the vast majority of the customers
   - The amount spent every month

   On a monthly basis, customers would all be queried on their satisfaction. If they give a 7-out-of-10 rating or higher, the monthly subscription counted. The new metric is: $\sum€7^+$, the total monthly subscription of all the 7^+ customers. To get more customers' feedback, they introduced two improvements. First, they would ask more bluntly for a figure between 1 and 10. The relationship managers and customer support employees of course also took notes on the details of this feedback. Next, to improve the interaction with the customers, they started to use tools like UserVoice to give the customers a more tangible platform where they could post ideas and change priorities of the product backlog.

3. Teams that are jointly responsible for handling support calls have chosen to decrease the number of calls per week per 1,000 customers. This KVI had to decrease to indicate success. By working together with, among other things, sales, IT, and marketing, they started to focus on reducing the number of unnecessary calls. This allowed the teams to give real attention to the customers who still call and give them a positive experience with the company. In other words, thanks to fewer calls, the teams could spend time on customers who really needed their attention and could focus on delivering customer impact.

1.2 HOW DO YOU FIND THE RIGHT KVIs?

A fuller plate doesn't make the food tastier.

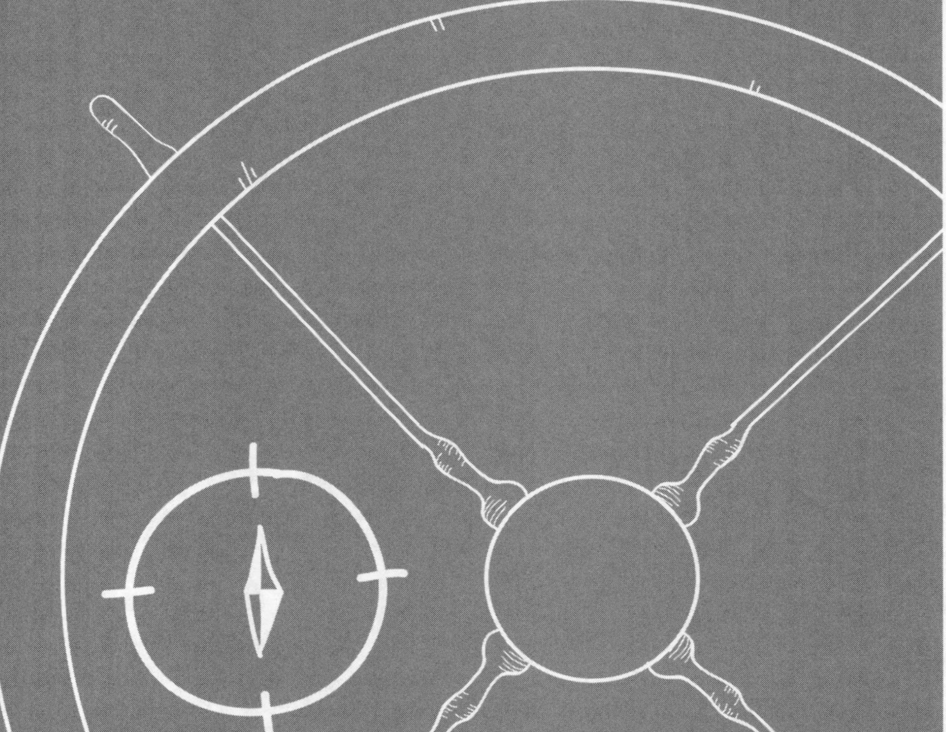

Introduction Questions

1. In which way are the metrics motivating the team to work smarter?
2. Which three customers are really more successful because of using the product?

Co-create
GOALS

What Is a Good KVI?

Gordon Ramsay is world famous for his cooking skills, books, films, and above all restaurant-consultancy skills. I spent hours watching the series *Hell's Kitchen* in which he helps restaurants to be successful again. He works with restaurants that provide poor quality, have customers walk away, are losing money, or for other reasons almost have to close their doors. In the course of a few days, he ensures that the restaurants can be successful again. Gordon saves many restaurant owners from bankruptcy, and they are very grateful to him. What makes him so unique and successful? Besides being an excellent chef and being able to coach people well (in my opinion), there is his unique skill that helps him to turn restaurants around again and again: he is focused on the needs of the customers who come to eat. As a result, he can make the restaurant a unique and popular place, and customers are happy to pay for that. This is how Gordon creates a customer impact that delivers value for the restaurant. It sounds easy, but in real life this is hard. There are so many things that blur the focus on the customer impact.

The basis of a successful restaurant is still relatively simple: delicious food, a full stomach, and a good atmosphere for a suitable price. His strength is to make these general concepts applicable to a specific restaurant because how he creates the positive customer impact for a restaurant is different every time. What is delicious food now? What is a good atmosphere for that neighborhood? What is a reasonable price for these guests? Gordon designs different recipes, a different restaurant format, and other prices depending on the specific situation. That makes him very agile: he is able to answer the client's needs each time. This allows him to respond to the specific situation, competition, target group, atmosphere, employees' capabilities, and much more. So every time, he creates a profitable formula. Many companies can learn from this—really focus on the basic needs of the customer, deliver impact, and turn that into value for the company. These three steps must be taken in order to craft a good KVI.

In Three Steps to a First KVI

So how do you develop and find a good KVI? Not by telling the people the new metric. This is often the traditional way of doing it, which isn't likely to support ownership, understanding, and collaboration. The new way is to co-create the metric. Together with a few people and a workshop, the first KVI is discovered. After a few months, this first version can be improved with new insight and experience.

The crafting of a good KVI consists of three steps that can be done in a workshop that is usually two to four hours. The steps in this workshop are as follows:

Step 1: Create a clear customer impact.

Step 2: Visualize how this creates value for the company.

Step 3: Define a metric that increases the focus on the customer.

Step 1: Create Clear Customer Impact

It starts with clarifying the customer impact for this situation. Clarify how the customer benefits by using the products or services. Does it give them a certain gain? For example, they are faster or happier, can realize their ambitions faster, or are more successful in a different way. Or does it relieve a certain pain? Does it help the customer spend less time on certain tasks, run less risk, or have less stress or hassle? The team members indirectly deliver a positive impact to their users by creating and improving products and services that are beneficial for them. Although the solutions may have changed and probably will change more quickly the next era, the underlying customer impact hasn't changed a bit. The way the customer impact is delivered is changing more and more quickly, but the underlying gains and pains hardly change.

I give two examples to explain this. The products and services around watching films at home have changed enormously in recent years. We do not go to a video store to rent videos; instead, we stream videos online from the couch. We watch Netflix and YouTube, we pause live TV, we easily record films from TV, and we watch movies in the park with the tablet—all examples of new products and services. The need for watching films for relaxation, romance, or whatever reason has not changed in recent years. The customer impact is and remains watching a movie. It is only that this customer impact is fulfilled in a totally different way. Blockbuster filed for bankruptcy in 2010[3] not because the underlying customer impact changed but because other companies could deliver the same customer impact easier and cheaper. Blockbuster probably steered on KPIs like the number of movies rented or the number of subscribers. Companies like Netflix and YouTube steer on KVIs like the number of movies actually watched. Because no matter what new technologies might surface in the future, we consumers continue to have the underlying need to relax and watch a movie. Successful companies are able to continue to respond to the stable needs of watching films with the help of new technologies and improved services.

Here is another example. Cars are bought for convenience, a feeling of freedom, cargo space, status, safety, or for taking a trip over the holidays. Various car brands profile themselves with a specific customer impact in their marketing campaigns, brochures, and appearance to be distinctive. Over the years, cars have changed and improved tremendously. New technologies, improved engines, and all kinds of other changes have made cars safer, faster, more economical, or easier. But the underlying needs of consumers have remained largely the same.

It is therefore important to focus on the customer impact. This is a key factor for teams in the dynamic market. But how does this customer impact generate money for the company, and does it contribute to continuity?

Step 2: Visualize the Tangible Value for the Company

If the customer's impact is clear, it can be made concrete how this brings value to the company. In this step, the entire business process is visualized: from harvesting new ideas and improvements to sketching solutions, building the best ideas, and gathering feedback

3. https://www.forbes.com/sites/gregsatell/2014/09/05/a-look-back-at-why-blockbuster-really-failed-and-why-it-didnt-have-to

from actual users. The self-managing agile teams need insight on this overall process and their role in it. Collectively, they brainstorm on how increasing the customer impact increases the value for the company. This value can only be optimized by collectively collaborating, sharing insights, and improving on feedback between all the teams involved. Is more food on the plate improving the value? Probably not. Improving the experience of the restaurant guests is more likely to improve the value. Is building more features in an app improving the value? Probably not; building those features that increase the DAU is more likely.

Table 1.1 presents some examples of the relationship between what teams do and the value for the company.

Table 1.1 Examples of the relationships between what the teams do and the value for the company

	Do	Products and Services	Customer impact	Value
Restaurant	Cook, serve, clean, welcome, handle reservations	Meals	Filled stomach, relaxation, romance for a fair price.	
Car manufacture	Designing and making car parts and mounting them to a car	Working cars	Faster from A to B. Or: status, luxury, safety.	Very happy and satisfied customers pay. Next they are ambassadors for the company.
Clothing manufacture	With cloth and other materials, design and build cloths	Cloth like trousers, blouses, and pants	Warm and neat. Or also: status, ego, first impression, luxury, or safety.	

Agile teams that have to continuously implement improvements must be innovative and have to work smarter. They can only do this if they have a clear picture of the complete process of value creation.

Step 3: Choose a Metric to Measure Value

If it is known how the work of the team increases the customer's impact and how this provides value for the company, the KVI can be chosen in the third step. Determining this metric is often a creative process, whereby it helps to combine the ideas of various employees into a concrete KVI. Often in this process, several KVIs are tried out for several months in order to make the KVI better and better.

How Do I Know We Have an Inspiring KVI?

Finding an inspiring KVI is also complex. It's a discovery. The first KVI is often not the right one, but setting a draft KVI and just experimenting with it is often the only way to find a better one. An inspirational KVI generates energy, motivates out-of-the-box thinking, and drives synergy. Sketching ideas and working with a certain KVI for several months will give the feedback and learnings to improve. This is the so-called *Sketch* → *Go* → *Learn* loop to discover the proper KVI.

But how does one know if they have found the right KVI? Experimenting and brainstorming with teams and customers on the following five *I*s results in practical guidelines for creating inspirational KVIs.

The 5×I for Inspirational KVIs

The 5×I (five *I*s) for inspirational KVIs include the following:

- **Influence.** The teams feel that they can influence the metric.
- **Insight.** The metric is tangible and visual. Team members update the metric themselves and are eager to know the latest numbers.
- **Ideas.** The metric causes ideas to thrive. It stimulates out-of-the-box thinking. Teams have a list of ideas, innovations, and disruptive features to improve.

- **Intent.** The intent behind the metric is also clear. The team members can explain the purpose or mission behind what they want to achieve.
- **Impact.** It focuses on the customer, and it can be explained to the customers or users that it serves them.

PITFALLS WHEN CHOOSING AND USING KVIs

Pitfalls when choosing and using KVIs include the following:

- **No feedback on choices made this week.** A KVI that is only measured a few times a year is not a good KVI because the choices today or this week are not reflected in the figures. This gives the team no insight to increase their self-management.
- **No influence.** Note that the team can influence the KVI. Some companies work with the wrong KVI, namely, the profit made. This clearly indicates the overall purpose and makes it measurable. However, the profit depends on many things, such as strategic depreciation and other accounting details. Often it is better to work with a margin calculation. Make it easy to calculate the margin of the different products and services, and use this as the KVI for the team.
- **Management dashboard only.** If the managers are only using the metric to know how the teams are doing, they know less than half the story. There could be all kinds of reasons why the KVI goes up and down, and these reasons are key lessons for the teams and the rest of the organization. Just associating the declining KVI with underperformance of the teams is the mindset of a noncomplex environment. There are numerous unknowns, dependencies, and external factors that influence the KVI. That's the beauty of it. Because only with the proactive brainpower, experience, and talents of everybody can we continuously find ways to positively influence the KVI. That makes it exciting, fun, and challenging. Talk with the teams and don't judge the numbers.
- **Waiting for the best possible KVI.** After studying the customer impact and how that brings value to the company, a superb KVI can be found. But if it takes weeks or months to implement it and to gather enough data to track

the KVI, it's probably still a bad KVI. A better way is to work with an existing metric and start gathering experience and learnings while the uber-KVI is implemented.

How Do I Give Inspiring Goals?

Often because the teams are part of the journey of finding the KVIs, they probably already feel connected with the goals. But not everybody was part of that journey. And as time passes, other people join. Therefore, successful leaders repeatedly ensure that the goals are clear and still inspiring. They know that inspiring goals are crucial because the job of the teams is often challenging. When searching for solutions, implementing improvements, and exceeding customer expectations, a lot of things are expected from the agile teams. It often takes a lot of energy and perseverance to achieve these goals. It is no longer about carrying out daily activities from 9 to 5, but about continuing to look for solutions creatively and searching elsewhere if these solutions initially do not work or when feedback from the customers is harsh.

But how do you ensure that these goals are inspiring? Over the years, I have been able to meet several inspiring agile leaders. They know how to get people moving, working together in teams and overcoming obstacles together. How do they do that? I have interviewed, observed, and had heart-to-heart chats with several agile leaders. Being inspiring is not a trick; true inspiration is about authenticity and vulnerability.

In addition, I discovered a few things that these successful agile leaders have in common when they speak to large or small groups:

1. **Dream.** They have a passion, an inspiring vision. They can explain their vision in such a way that it becomes very tangible and relatable. This gives the teams the trust and the energy to go for it.
2. **Customer focus.** This dream is not internal to the company but oriented toward the customer. The focus is on what teams can mean to customers and how they can have a positive impact.

3. **Vulnerability.** Agile leaders show courage by being vulnerable to large groups. They indicate that they can't do it themselves and that they do not have all the answers. They are imperfect, and they make mistakes. But they act not out of uncertainty, but out of authenticity.
4. **Exploration.** They do not present a detailed plan, but a voyage of discovery and exploration. They outline in their own words that it is too complex and unpredictable to know what exactly is needed to be successful. They can't give any guarantees about what exactly is going to happen or how it will look in detail. The call is to help each other and not to go for self-interest or short-term solutions.
5. **Pain.** They are honest about the effort and the pain it will cost in the coming period. It will not be an easy path, and setbacks are part of it.

In many cases it came down to courage. Agile leaders could have postponed the change, continuing to do what they always did. That would have led to less risk and pain in the short run. But they stuck their necks out and chose to inspire. They wanted to turn around the way customers were served and the way the talents and opportunities of employees were utilized. This ultimately led to a change that yielded more than just company results. In many cases, employees started to believe in themselves, and customers were satisfied with the products and services supplied.

It is the agile leader's job to ensure that each team has that clear and inspiring focus on what they need to *achieve*. In practice, this means ensuring that the team understands why products and services are of interest to customers and how this generates value for the company.

1.3 HOW TO VISUALIZE THE CUSTOMER IMPACT?

I would define Amazon by our big ideas, which are [customer-centric], putting the customer at the center of everything we do.

– Jeff Bezos, CEO, Amazon

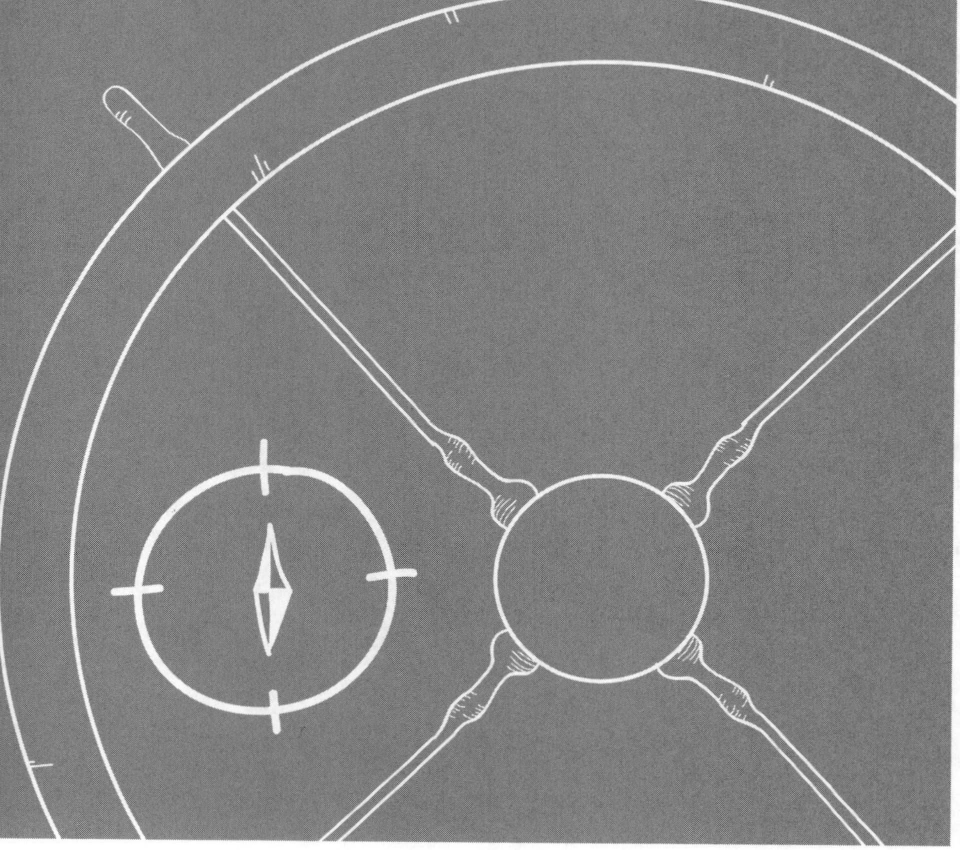

INTRODUCTION QUESTIONS

1. What makes the customers of your company more successful?
2. In which way is making the customers more successful a motivation for your teams and department?

Farmdrone

Matthew founded a startup company for developing a new a sophisticated drone to help farmers in gathering insight in their crops. He wanted to support farmers so they didn't have to travel throughout their land and check the status of the crops but could get a daily update without leaving the house. The drone would fly over the crops and gather all kinds of data. It would save time and give more accurate insight because the drone could check more land in less time than the farmer with his tractor.

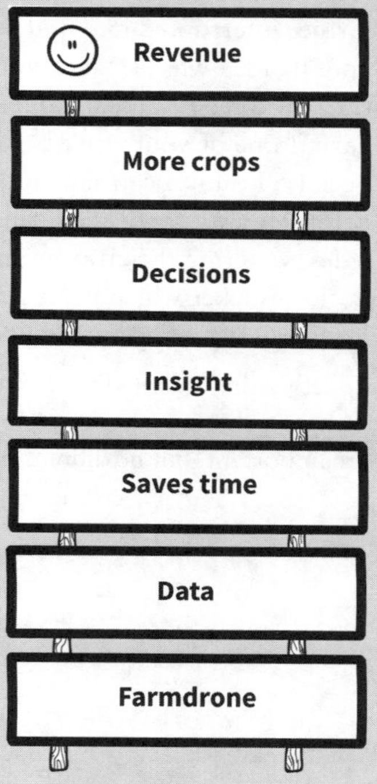

Figure 1.3 How the Farmdrone relates to the customer impact

He was searching for investors to realize this product. After pitching the idea, many investors weren't enthusiastic because they couldn't believe the drone would be either accurate enough or worth buying. Early calculations would make the drone very expensive and investors didn't think it would be bought by farmers.

Hearing all the feedback from the investors, he started to doubt his idea. He gave it some thought and took another look at his notes. His notes were all about the technical details of the drone, the requirements of the battery, the wind speed it could deal with, the algorithm for the optimal autopilot routes, and how the drone could get regular software updates. He was pretty proud of his technical analysis. He also discussed these details with farmers, and many farmers agreed with his specifications.

So why couldn't he convince many investors? Matthew thought about it and looked again at his problem. He made a list of why his drone was helpful.

He made a stack of seven blank pieces of paper in front of him. At the bottom he wrote "Farmdrone" (see Figure 1.3). He looked at his product from the perspective of the farmer and asked himself why the farmer would buy his product. Because it gives him *Data*. Why would he want to have data in a different way? Because it *Saves time*. What could the farmer do more quickly? It gives him quicker *Insight*. Why is this insight of benefit? Because he could make *Decisions*. Why would that help the farmer? Because it increases the production of his crops. Matthew wrote "More crops" on the piece of paper. Why would the farmer want more crops? The answer is easy: because it increases revenue and makes the farmer more successful.

He looked at the list and was pretty proud of the result. He called one of the farmers he already contacted about this idea and asked if they could have a cup of coffee and look at his results.

A few days later, he sat with the farmer. Matthew was pretty excited. He explained to the farmer what he did, but the farmer didn't look so happy during his explanation. The farmer interrupted him and asked, do you know how we farmers make profit? Have you got any idea what it takes to make profit in the end? Matthew thought he knew, but he started to see he actually didn't. The farmer explained: "The reason I'm interested in this Farmdrone of yours isn't because it saves me time; it's a totally different reason. It's because I think I can save a lot of money on crops that won't make it." Matthew didn't get it. He waited for the farmer to explain. "We farmers spend a lot of money on pesticides, watering the crops in the dry periods, and all kinds of nutrition. I expect that I can decide quicker which parts I can *write off* and not invest any money in. The cost will be a lot lower, while the harvest will be probably be the same."

Together they adapted the list Matthew created earlier, and they added a few pieces of paper. Matthew thought about it, and he discovered he was focusing on the details of the drone, which are important, but he didn't fully understood how his product would benefit the customers.

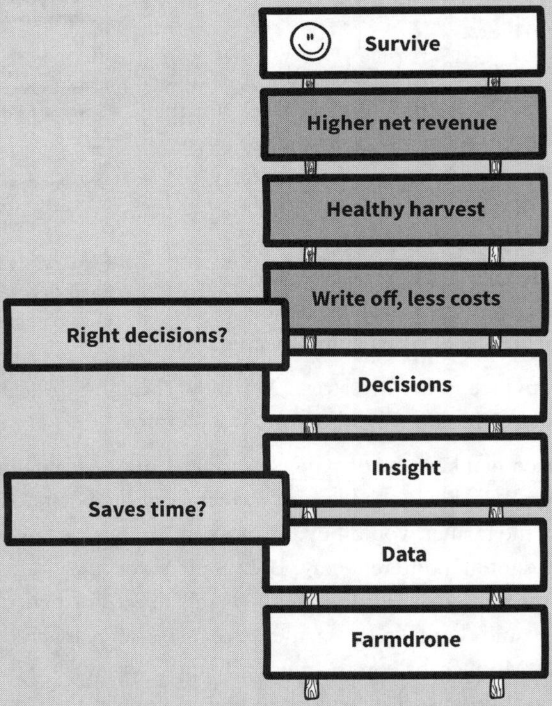

Figure 1.4 Why the Farmdrone really has a positive customer impact

Next they brainstormed further and talked about the risks—not the risks of the product, such as whether the battery was big enough, or whether the drone was intelligent enough to find his routes. They talked about the risks for the *farmer.* His friend explained that he saw two important risks: would the drone gather at least the same insight in less time, and would it gather preferably better insight? So "Save time" was changed to a different type of note because it was an odd item in the overall list. And the other risk was whether the farmer would make the right decisions, based on the insight of the drone, to write off the correct crops. These two risks were actually assumptions that would hugely affect the success of the drone. Would farmers actually make better decisions that increased the overall net revenue? See Figure 1.4.

Matthew drove home and thought about the things he had discovered. He could see why his potential investors weren't so enthusiastic about his product. It wasn't because of an issue with the technical ingenuity, but because none of them (including Matthew) really understood the customer impact. He phoned a few of his potential investors and started to explain the customer side of his product.

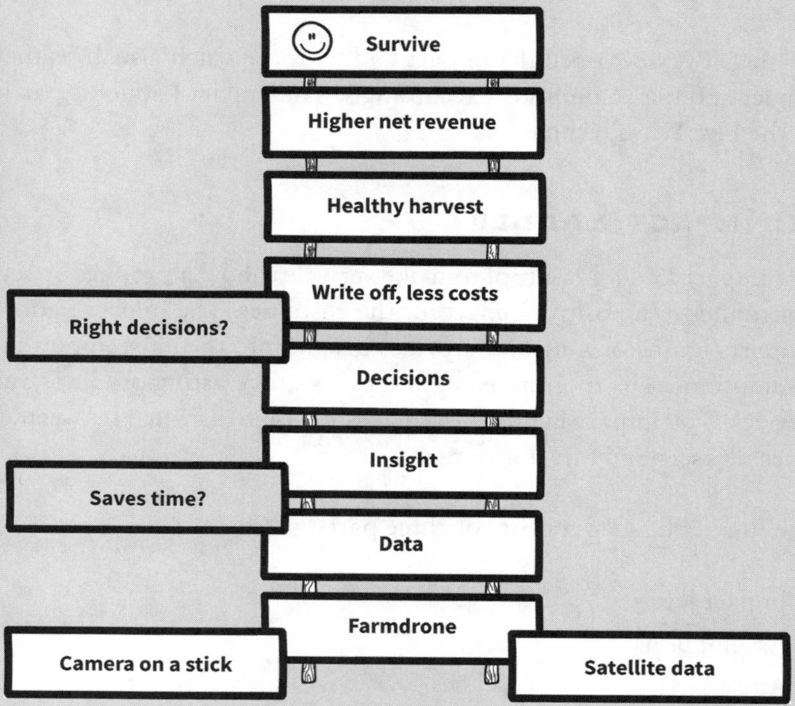

Figure 1.5 Alternatives for the Farmdrone

While talking to one of his potential investors and brainstorming on the assumptions, the investor asked, "Is there a quicker way to validate our assumptions without building a drone?" Matthew's immediate response was almost a big no, but then he thought about it. There are quicker ways to get the data. Why not use a dummy-drone like a big camera on a stick or use satellite data images and data? He extended his overview with some alternatives. The end result is illustrated in Figure 1.5.

COMPLEX CUSTOMER IMPACT

In real life, it can be difficult to clearly understand the customer impact, especially when the customer is another company. Many teams think that they know the customer impact because they don't know what they don't know. To give these teams the right goals and to give them a proper KVI, it must be clear how the product delivers value to the customer. Successful agile leaders make sure that the agile teams really understand how they are beneficial for the customer.

For that, I've developed the Impact Ladder tool, which visualizes the customer impact and the assumptions accordingly. The Impact Ladder is partly based on the Five Whys technique.[4]

TOOL 2: IMPACT LADDER

The Impact Ladder is a tool to make very clear how a product or service contributes to a positive impact for the customer. The Impact Ladder supports brainstorming and provides insight into the most important assumptions. The tool can be used for new and existing products and services. The Impact Ladder also makes it easier to switch between different types of users and target groups.

The Impact Ladder consists of three parts:

1. Impact levels
2. Assumptions
3. Alternatives

4. Serrat, O. 2017. The Five Whys Technique. In *Knowledge Solutions*. Springer, Singapore.

Schematically, the Impact Ladder looks like Figure 1.6.

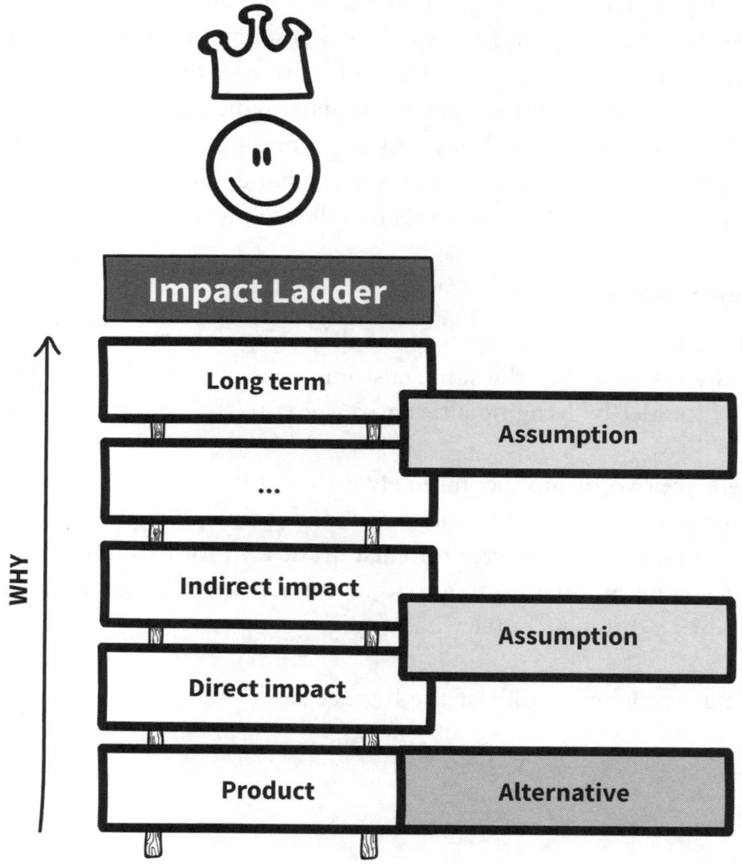

Figure 1.6 Impact Ladder

Impact Levels

The impact levels show step by step how a product or service contributes to the success of the customer. The direct impact starts with the use: convenience, reliability, and time savings. A few levels higher is often cheaper or better. And another few levels higher, the strategic advantage and long-term results can be found.

ASSUMPTION

If the impact levels have been added to the Impact Ladder, the assumptions can be displayed. Figure 1.6 visualizes that an assumption is always between two consecutive impact levels. Examples are whether the product actually saves time or whether the costs are actually reduced. These assumptions are actually risks, often called business risks, and must be properly monitored during the development of the product. Changes, innovations, and experiments should be monitored to validate the assumptions.

ALTERNATIVES

Finally, there are alternative ways of delivering impact because there are often several ways to realize the same customer impact. This is visualized in the Impact Ladder by hanging alternatives next to the relevant impact level.

If there are two or more completely different branches in customer groups, not just one Impact Ladder can be made for this. In that case, a separate Impact Ladder works better for each branch. If, for example, the drone is also used for other industries, like road maintenance or life guards, each target group has a different Impact Ladder.

There are more examples of the Impact ladder on www.tval.nl.

Summary of Part 1—Co-Create Goals

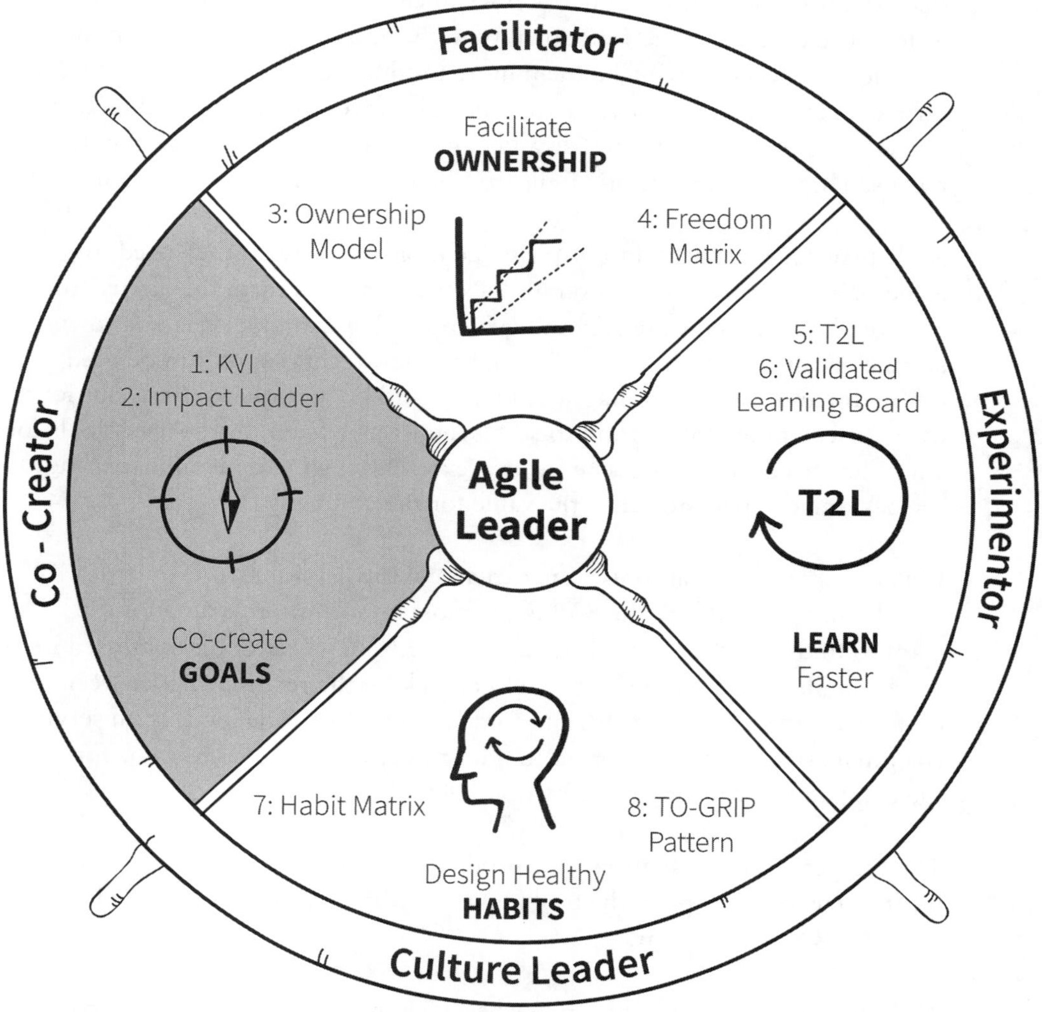

This first part of the steering wheel explained how the agile leader can co-create goals. See the figure above for an overview of this part of the toolkit. Agile teams operate in a complex environment. Markets, technologies, competitors, and customers' wishes change so quickly and so unpredictably that teams need a new type of goals to give them direction. In static or slow-changing markets, the performance of employees and teams can be measured relatively easily by measuring the output. An employee or team that produces more has a higher performance than others. But agile teams are different. Delivering more functionality in the app or handling more phone calls doesn't necessarily make them more productive. Therefore, they need a different set of goals to measure their performance and give them direction. These new goals make it tangible and concrete what "winning the game" means. These goals, therefore, indicate when teams are really successful.

Agile teams need a clear and inspiring goal regarding what they need to achieve. This focuses on the overall objective and gives them the ability to change plans when unexpected things happen. For example, it is unknown in advance what the competition will do, how new technologies can be used optimally, and what the dynamics in teams will be. In order to find solutions, to embrace opportunities, and to seek synergy as a team, teams need goals for what they need to achieve. The focus is external; it should be on increasing the customer impact and thus the value for the company.

In Part 1, two practical tools were explained: the key value indicator (KVI) and the Impact Ladder. The KVI is the most important indicator for the team to find out whether they are generating value. The tool is expressed in a single number, visualized in a trend line, making the relationship between customer impact and value for the company tangible. The focus is on serving customers smarter and better, so that customers generate more value for the company—achieving more by doing less.

The Impact Ladder visualizes how products and services contribute to a positive customer impact: the tool makes the difficult and complicated customer's situation clear.

The other three parts of the steering wheel reinforce this co-creating goals part. Part 2, "Facilitate Ownership," will offer further practicality on how the teams can become proactive, proud, and energized. In Part 3, "Learn Faster," we'll discover that tools like T2L are crucial if the teams are looking at recent data. Part 4, "Design Healthy Habits," gives the goals a healthy atmosphere and culture.

The Agile Leader as a Co-Creator of Inspiring Goals

In complex and quickly changing markets, it's hard to know the perfect goal. Co-creating the goal with the teams serves the agile leader in three ways. First, the goal will probably be better because more people put thought into it. Second, the teams will know the "why" behind the goal, and if the goal needs to be changed or improved, the teams will come up with proposals and ideas. Last but not least, the teams will likely be more inspired to work on a goal they co-created than on a goal that is bestowed upon them. When searching for solutions, implementing improvements, and exceeding customer expectations, we expect a lot from the agile teams. It often takes a lot of energy and perseverance to grow as a team and achieve the goals. It is no longer about carrying out daily activities from 9 to 5, but rather about looking for solutions creatively. And, if these solutions initially do not work, it is about continuing to solve issues as a team. That is why it is important that the agile leader gets better and better in his role as a co-creator. That she asks for feedback in her motivational skills, she learns, and she grows. Finding and improving the inspirational environment for the teams is a discovery. Sketching a first version of the tools and learning as we go is the only way to continuously improve the tools and environment.

Knowing whether the teams have an inspiring goal, the following five *I*s can be used to gather feedback.

- **Influence.** Do the teams feel that they can influence the metric?
- **Insight.** Is the goal tangible and visual? Do team members update the metrics themselves and are they eager to know the latest numbers?
- **Ideas.** Does it cause ideas to thrive? It should stimulate out-of-the-box thinking. Teams can have a list of ideas, innovations, and disruptive features to improve.
- **Intent.** Is the intent behind the goal also clear? Can the team members explain the purpose or mission behind what they want to achieve?
- **Impact.** Does it focus on the customer?

CONCRETE ACTIONS

The following are some examples of actions to put the tools, examples, and ideas from Part 1 into practice.

1. Share ambitions and dreams more often—both your own and those of others. Practice and grow in inspiring and sharing each other's passions.
2. Ask for examples of successful customers. Did agile teams deliver concrete customer impact in recent times? If so, share. If not, work together to find ideas about how to improve.
3. Make an overview of the teams and their KVIs. This makes it known which teams have a concrete KVI and which teams still need help with this.

Notes

PART 2
Facilitate Ownership

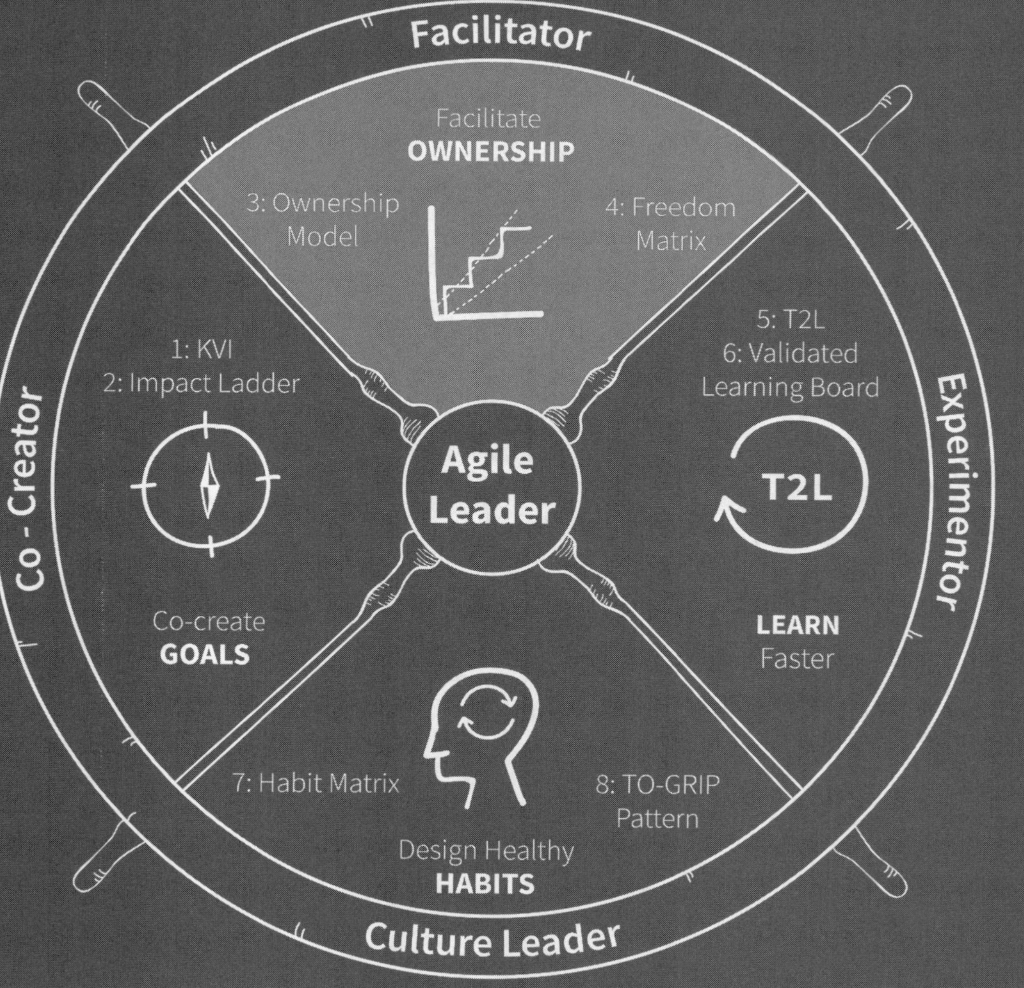

2.1 WHEN DO TEAMS TAKE OWNERSHIP?

Dispirited, unmotivated, unappreciated workers cannot compete in a highly competitive world.

– Frances Hesselbein

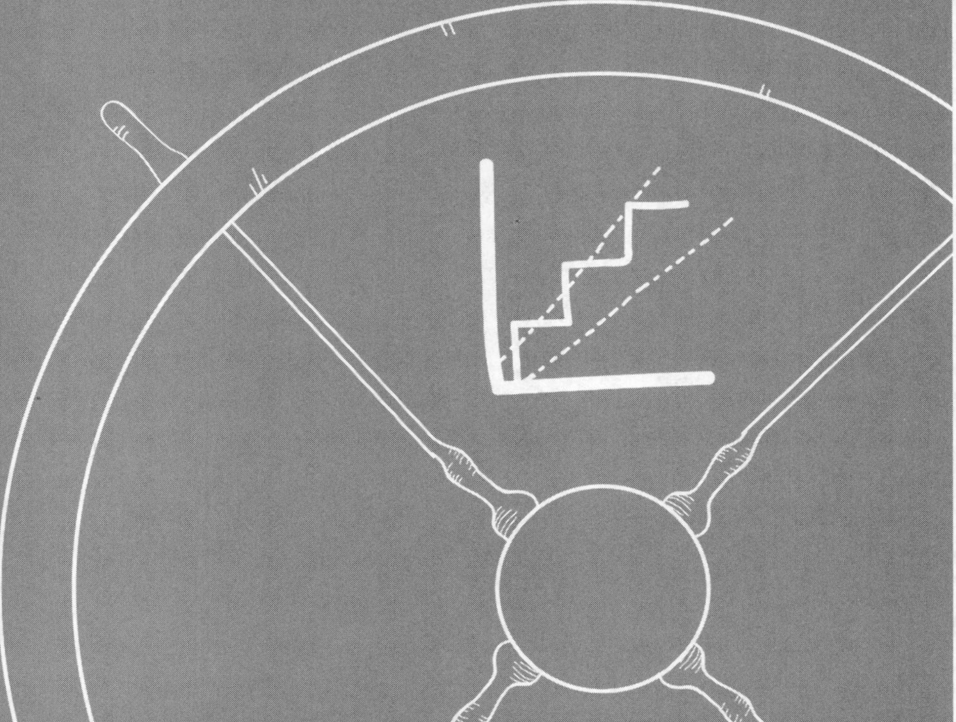

Introduction Questions

1. How would you define ownership?
2. What are situations where you lose ownership quickly?

Introduction

It's Monday morning. Patricia arrives in the office to find her teams busy at work. Some notice her arrival, smile, and nod, but most are engrossed in their work. A few people are gathered around a whiteboard, lost in discussion. Two others are paired up in front of a screen, analyzing the latest website conversion data, and several others are talking about their weekends in the kitchen area. The office has an energy; everyone is engaged, and their body language clearly says that they like working together. Seeing this makes Patricia feel good.

A year ago, when she came to work as a manager in this department, things were very different: the teams had no energy, no passion, and no can-do attitude. Almost everyone was passive, just doing his job and trying to go home just a bit earlier. When she asked a question, team members seemed to be trying to keep their mouths shut as long as possible. When committed schedules were not met, people just shrugged with resignation; no one felt empowered to do anything about it. Their results were poor, but no one seemed to care or offered ideas for improvement.

Her predecessor had stripped the teams of pride, initiative, and creativity. Patricia knew she had to turn the situation around, but it would take a while before she could win the trust of the team members, who were overburdened with procedures, daily checklists, and unrealistic (and wrongly focused) targets. Her predecessor had made the goal focusing on filling in checklists and following procedures, and he berated people who failed to comply, even when they were doing the right thing. When team members did what they felt was right thing, they never received recognition. Team members were demotivated and beaten down. Patricia believed that they were skilled enough to do their work independently. In fact, the procedures never matched the complexity of their work; checklists didn't reflect the diagnostic, dynamic nature of the work, and team members themselves had much better ideas to prevent mistakes and to learn continuously. Having checklists meant that employees did not look for creative solutions, but in order to be successful, creativity was essential. Only by working together, taking initiative, and implementing improvements would they be successful. Patricia knew that she would never be smart enough on her own to think of everything in advance. She needed all the thinking, experience, and talent of every team member to succeed.

Patricia decided try something new. A few weeks after she started, she called all the employees together. She explained what she had noticed and what she planned to do in the near future. Each team went through a program. After a short training, team building, and workshop, teams would be fully autonomous. There would be no more checklists and procedures. From that day on, team members had complete freedom to plan and coordinate their own work. They became responsible for their holiday schedules, knowledge transfer, and hiring new employees. They had to give each other feedback, and by the end of the year the team would even conduct the requisite assessment interviews themselves. In the first instance, this resulted in a lot of enthusiasm and energy in the department. The first teams started successfully. But after a few weeks, the change did not continue, and then, slowly, the teams slipped back into their old behaviors: they became passive again, resumed their grumbling, and the results went down the drain. There was no lasting drive, no passion, and no ownership in the teams. Patricia was distraught. What had she done wrong? What did she overlook?

In hindsight, that was one of the toughest moments of her career. She believed in her department and the new way of working, and yet the expected improvement did not come true. In order to save the department, she had to partially curtail the given freedom and thus roll back part of the change. This broke the little confidence and trust she had just built up with many people. The promised and long-awaited freedom faded, and reminders of the previous manager came alive. Fortunately, something special happened: Some teams did thrive, strangely enough. Proactivity and ownership emerged, and teams started to organize their work themselves, implement improvements, and share knowledge! At first, Patricia did not understand why and questioned several employees about this strange effect. She received feedback that the clarity, improved structure, and reduced freedom were exactly what the teams needed. Within these new borders they could actually do their work better!

This is how Patricia came to see the key to success: in order to stimulate passion, proactivity, and ownership in the teams, they do not just need a lot of freedom. Rather, they needed just enough freedom to match their maturity, and actually just a little bit more. She discovered that managing teams can be compared to raising her children. If she let her daughter of 8 years live by herself, her daughter might like that very much in the beginning—but soon chaos would result, causing huge problems and bad consequences that her daughter would not like at all because her daughter would get much more freedom than her maturity could handle. Patricia began to see that the same was true for her teams: they needed exactly that freedom that encourages them to grow without resulting in chaos and lack of control. Because only at this level of freedom does passion, energy, buzz, perseverance, and entrepreneurial spirit arise and grow. At this level of freedom, team members inspire each other to share knowledge, learn, serve customers better, and cooperate intensively. This sort of behavior and energy is exactly what Patricia sees today as she looks around her, and it is so contagious that it puts a smile on her face.

What Is Ownership?

When I use the term *ownership,* I mean that teams pick up ownership voluntarily and take responsibility for the results of a product or service. These teams are proactive and have the passion and energy to really make an impact for the users of their product. They work together, give each other feedback, exhibit resilience, are open minded, and learn continuously. They also help other teams to grow. As entrepreneurs, they take ownership of both the strategy and the way it is implemented. In addition, they realize that they own their own challenges, solutions, and customers. The product or service feels like their own child in a beautiful way. This gives teams pride, creativity, energy, passion, and satisfaction in their work.

Ownership The mental state of a team when they feel accountable for their results. They have chosen to pick up this ownership freely and autonomously. They organize their work proactively, are transparent to each other, and continuously improve. They seek solutions and collaboration and are not searching for excuses.

Ownership cannot be imposed or enforced. It is the voluntary choice of the team to take ownership because being forced does not coincide with passion, energy, and fun. It must be granted by the leader to give the teams the ability to take ownership. It must of course also be rewarded and sustained.

Why Ownership?

When the work is complex, when teams have to grow continuously, and when employees have to find creative solutions every day to really help customers, something special is needed to be successful. When every situation, challenge, and customer is too unique, people need to be empowered to think and decide for themselves. Ownership ensures that they think outside the box to come up with innovative solutions that really help customers. In case of unexpected problems, difficult challenges, or when things go wrong, ownership ensures that teams feel responsible to solve this. They don't have to wait for others to come up with solutions. When they feel ownership, they don't blame others for their challenges. Even when it gets tough, these teams continue to look for solutions and find opportunities. This is crucial because in complex environments, solutions can only be found by exploring and experimenting, learning from failures, and continuously growing as a team. Ownership gives them momentum to overcome unexpected challenges and obstacles.

As a leader, it's wonderful to see teams take ownership. Not only is this often the only way to be successful, but it also gives a deep sense of satisfaction to leaders. It's the agile leader's job to create an environment in which people and teams grow, work together, laugh, build trust, and do beyond-exceptional things for the customers. Micromanaging—telling people which tasks they have to do and making all kinds of small decisions—is not only too slow in this rapid world, but it also doesn't bring out the best in people. It often kills their brainpower, their creativity, and the synergy within the teams. Again: agile leaders create a working environment in which employees thrive and let them be proud on their work.

> *It's the agile leader's job to create an environment in which people and teams grow, work together, laugh, build trust, and feel proud on the things they do for their customers.*

How Do Teams Deal with Ownership?

How can an agile leader get his teams to take ownership of their work? They can't be forced into it; they must voluntarily take it on. The agile leader can only create an inspiring environment and encourage ownership, giving teams exactly enough freedom to suit their own maturity—no more, no less.

To give teams the right degree of freedom, the agile leader must know when to intervene and when not to. If he acts too quickly, he gives his team too little freedom, causing them to feel frustrated or thwarted. Teams in these circumstances will not take ownership. If the leader doesn't intervene or if he intervenes too late, his team gets too much freedom, resulting in the team feeling lost and confused; they also will not take on ownership.

How does a leader recognize situations in which he has to let go and other situations in which he should intervene and take action? Agile leaders struggle with this because every team is different, and teams are also constantly changing and growing. Striking the right balance means answering the following five questions:

1. When is intervening the best strategy, and when is letting go better?
2. How mature is my team?
3. How do typical teams grow?
4. How can the borders be aligned with the maturity?
5. When does the ownership model work and when does it not?

To help answer these questions, the third and fourth tools from the agile leadership toolkit are useful: the Ownership Model, which visualizes what teams need to take genuine ownership, and the Freedom Matrix, which makes concrete what specific freedom a team has, and when. More about these shortly. First, I'll explain the role of the agile leader as facilitator.

The Agile Leader as a Facilitator

The role of the agile leader in this second part of is that of a facilitator. A facilitator is someone who actively supports a group or team in achieving a result. A facilitator helps in getting to understand the common goal and also in planning to reach the desired goal. Again, ownership can't be forced on the team. Ownership can't be created by telling (or yelling at) the team that they have to take ownership. Successful agile leaders ask their teams what they need in order to take ownership voluntarily. Vulnerable and passionate, they share their motivation regarding why they want their teams to take ownership—not for the ego or the power but because they know how crucial ownership is in this complex world.

It's crucial that the tools explained in this part are used from a facilitator mindset. By improving the environment in which the teams operate, the leader can actively improve the ownership and thereby the success of the teams. But to know what to change in the environment, he has to ask for candor in what the teams need. What needs to be changed, added, or removed? Do, for example, they need more or less decision power on certain topics? Do they need to hire a certain expertise? Do they need training or mentoring on a certain topic? Does another team have to be told they deliver a product that is too low quality?

When, on the other hand, the leader assumes what the teams need, he has a small chance of being right. Also, copying what worked for another team is not the way to engage ownership.

By asking openly what the teams need to grow ownership—and by doing so, facilitating ownership—the agile leader can actually create an environment with awesome teams that operate on high levels of proactiveness, pride, creativity, and results that are beyond expectations.

Skills the leader can develop to improve the craft of facilitating are as follows:

- **Powerful questions.** Powerful questions increase creativity, promote honesty and transparency, stimulate out-of-the-box thinking, and focus on the outcome. By asking powerful questions, the teams are invited to take action, discover solutions, and make things clear and explicit. Nonpowerful questions are often aggressive, blaming, or directing to a fixed solution. These nonpowerful questions stimulate a can't-do mindset, making of excuses, resistance to change, or unfairness. The difference between powerful questions and offering help is often that the helper (the person asking the questions) is doing most of the problem solving and the actual work to fix it. Conversely, good powerful questions give the teams the feeling they can also solve the challenges at hand. Examples of powerful questions are
  - What are the possibilities?
  - What seems to confuse you?
  - What are other angles you can think of?
  - If you could do it over again, what would you do differently?
- **Self-reflection.** The behavior of the teams is a mirror of the environment agile leaders create. Nobody comes to his work thinking, "Today I want to be demotivated, criticize others, and distrust my boss." When people don't

have that spark in their eye called ownership, it's not because they want it to be that way. It's because we agile leaders haven't yet improved the environment enough. Improving the environment starts with a moment of self-reflection as an agile leader. In other words, being a better facilitator of ownership goes hand in hand with being better at reflecting on one's own behavior. What did I do wrong? What can I do different? What do I need to do less (or more) so my teams pick up ownership? Do I have the courage to be vulnerable and candid enough to tell the teams that I need their feedback on how I lead?

- **Team process.** Good teams reflect, modify, and amplify each other's ideas into even better ideas, seeking synergies to produce a better result. Together they are smarter than the team members are individually. Building these awesome teams is a difficult skill to master. The model I often use is the model of the five dysfunctions of a team by Patrick Lencioni.[1] It explains perfectly what teams need in order to grow from individuals to a high-performing team. The second level, "fear of conflict," is particularly interesting—inspiring, but also hard.
- **Growth of craftsmanship among team members.** People in successful agile teams are multiskilled, which means they master different areas of expertise. They need an environment that not only promotes knowledge transfer and skill development but also inspires them to become true craftsmen at several areas of expertise. Agile teams that develop software need craftsmen in their teams on expertises such as continuous deployment, performance test automation, or cybersecurity. Teams in marketing need craftsmen on social media, SEO, lead generation automation, or emotion marketing. As an agile leader, it's impossible to be the expert on all the areas of expertise a team will need. Therefore, successful agile leaders ask what teams need to grow their skills, and they use this information to improve the environment of the teams. So, teams work in an environment where they can become masters in their area of expertise and start becoming experts in new areas as needed.

1. https://www.tablegroup.com/books/dysfunctions

2.2 WHEN IS INTERVENING THE BEST STRATEGY, AND WHEN IS LETTING GO BETTER?

To let go or not to let go,
that is the question.

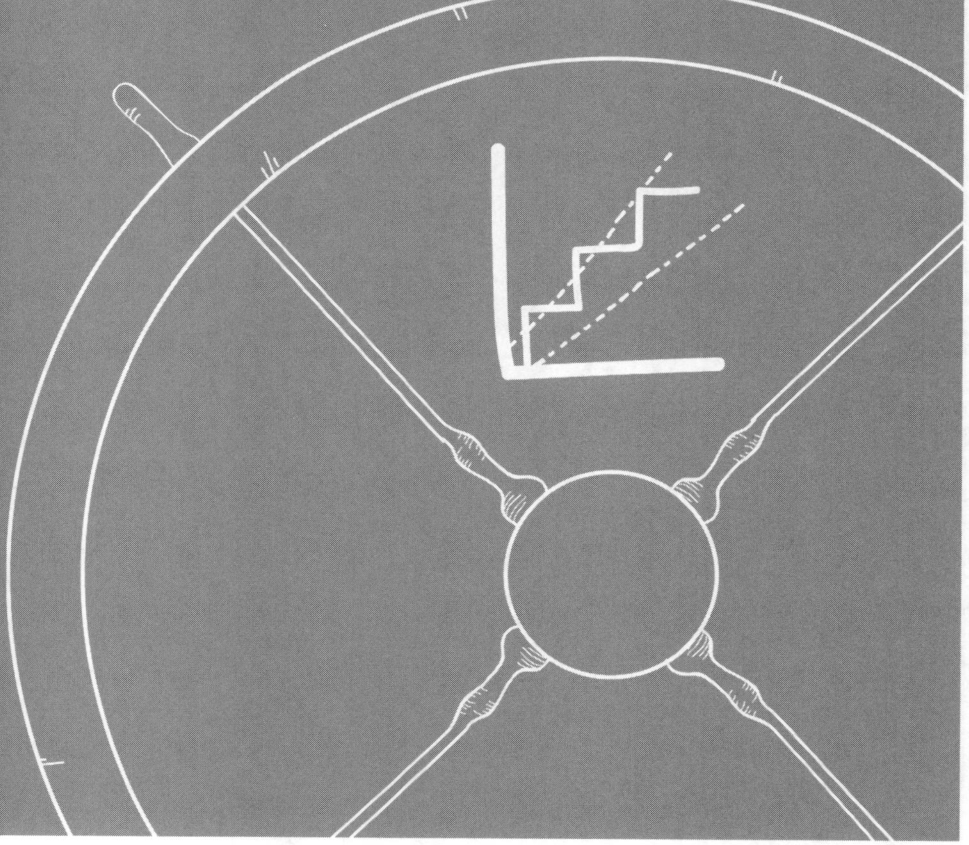

Introduction Questions

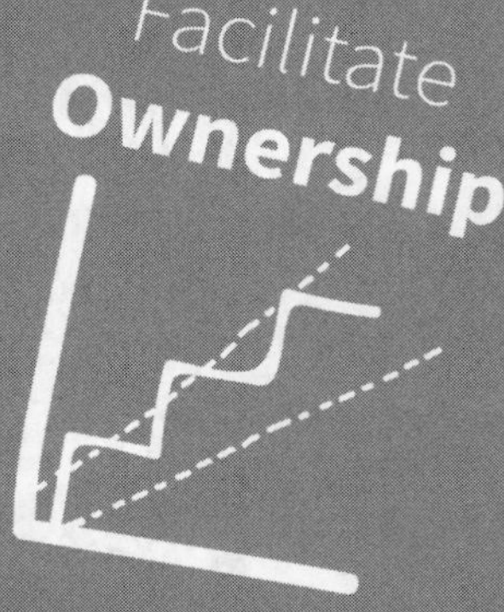

1. Which teams provide a real example in taking ownership? What behaviors do they demonstrate?
2. Do you tend to intervene too quickly or let go too much? How do you know how best to interact?

If the manager properly balances his interventions and does nothing (sitting on his hands, not intervening), the teams will take ownership. However, it's hard to always know exactly what to do. If the team delivers a low-quality result, should you act? Should you intervene when a team does not come up with solutions on its own? And what if talented employees leave the team? Or if customers or stakeholders complain about the results? Should you intervene when you think the team is about to make a major mistake? When should you do nothing? How do you give teams the space to learn and grow?

Whether or not it's wise to intervene depends on the maturity of the team. A highly mature team can independently organize their work and achieve great results, but a team just starting still needs a lot of help, guidance, and support. If the team is very mature and the agile leader gives little freedom and often intervenes, the team will become frustrated and passive; they will no longer come up with solutions themselves. Good people will leave, and if they don't, they will just passively do what they are told to do. Low quality and high risk will result. The team actually needs more space, and the manager should let go a lot more.

On the other hand, it also does not work if a newly formed team still figuring out how to collaborate (a *starting team*) gets too much freedom from the manager. The team feels lost; they do not know exactly what they have to do, and they can't assess the risks themselves. The team itself cannot come up with solutions on their own because they lack sufficient knowledge. This, too, results in good people leaving. The people who stay experience frustration from the lack of clarity, and they slip into passivity, also resulting in low quality and high risk. Although the results are the same, the team needs less space, and the manager must intervene by increasing the borders and offering concrete help.

To know when to let go and when to step in is a daunting challenge. Based purely on signals of passivity, low quality, employees who leave, and lack of improvement, the agile leader can't know whether intervention or letting go is best; he must first know the maturity of the team to know how much freedom they need in order to take ownership. But the big question is: how do you know the maturity of the team? Can the team members decide that for themselves? How can the manager know for certain? Experience has shown that the answer can only be found by talking about it together. The Ownership Model helps to facilitate this discussion, making it clear whether intervention is necessary or whether to let go is the better option.

TOOL 3: OWNERSHIP MODEL

The Ownership Model visualizes the relationship between the freedom and the maturity of the team. It consists of two axes, two bad zones, a good zone, and a staircase. Only when the freedom and maturity of the teams are in balance can the teams take ownership (see Figure 2.1).

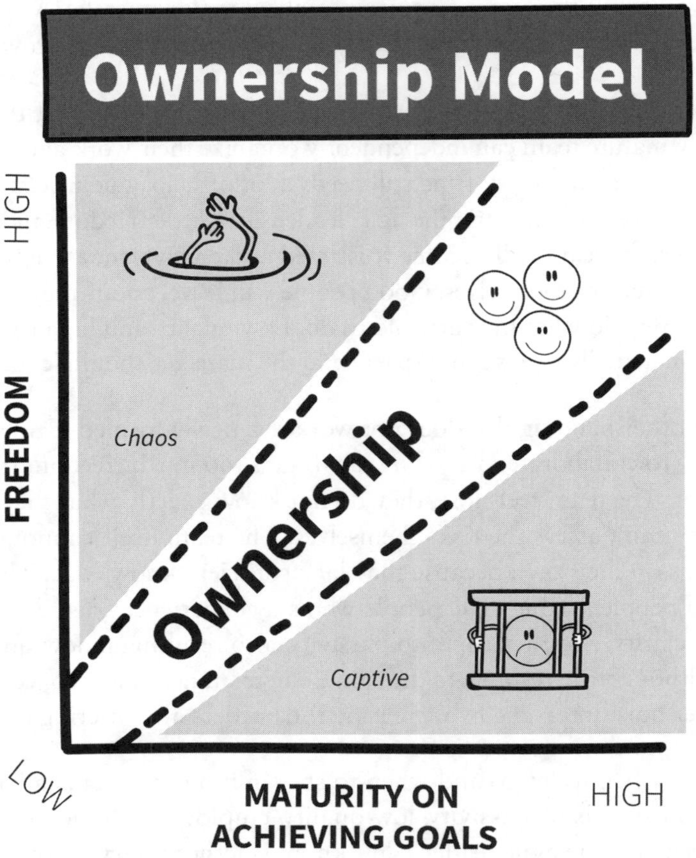

Figure 2.1 The Ownership Model

HORIZONTAL AXIS: MATURITY ON ACHIEVING GOALS

Maturity indicates the extent to which a team is independently capable of organizing their work to deliver valuable products and services to customers, and the extent to which the team can self-organize their customer impact.

A highly mature team can

- Plan and align their own work
- Deliver quality products and services to their customer(s)
- Continuously improve their own processes
- Get feedback from customers to increase their impact
- Collaborate autonomously with the rest of the organization
- Give each other feedback to increase their own craftsmanship and competence

Contrast this with a low-maturity team who still needs help from their agile leader to achieve these same results. A low-maturity team will still need the agile leader to guide them in matters such as planning and aligning their work, making team agreements, arranging the holiday schedule, giving each other feedback, and managing the stakeholders.

Vertical Axis: Freedom

Freedom describes the degree of independence from the agile leader that the teams exhibit. With a low level of freedom, they need alignment and approval for many issues, and they are given many details upfront. With a high level of freedom, they can arrange things independently.

For example, teams with a high degree of freedom may

- Make many decisions themselves and also bear the consequences
- Manage their own stakeholders
- Continuously improve the process and the cooperation with the other teams themselves
- Solve their own impediments and challenges
- Continue to operate within the boundaries of the rest of the organization

Freedom is accompanied by responsibility and consequences. When a leader—with the best intentions—removes the negative consequences of the team's own choices, the team will exhibit less ownership because they no longer bear the responsibility of their own behavior. When they are not held accountable for their choices or do not bear the consequences of their actions, they will not feel the collective pain as a team, they will not improve as quickly, and their growth will lag behind. Their capacities will also not be fully exercised. If this continues for a long time, they will lose their capacity for ownership.

To illustrate the situation in which a team has a lot of freedom and they bear the consequences for their actions, consider the following example of a highly mature Customer Contact team who gave bad advice to a customer, resulting in an extremely dissatisfied customer. In the past, the manager would have handled this, apologizing and searching for a solution. Now, the team solved the mistake themselves: they decided that to compensate the customer they would provide a discount on a product that the customer needed, which satisfied the customer. In order to give this discount, they did not have to get permission. Because the team could remedy their mistake independently, their confidence and sense of ownership grew; they were proud of how they solved the problem and thought of solutions to prevent this in the future. Despite the fact that they had to work harder to correct the consequences, their energy and pride rose.

Two Bad Zones

The two bad zones occur when freedom and maturity are not in balance.

- **Too much freedom: Chaos.** If the team is given more freedom than matches their maturity, they won't take ownership. They feel lost, and with too many opportunities and uncertainties, they lack the perspective to make effective choices. Because they can't adequately anticipate the consequences of their choices, it ends up in chaos. As a consequence, they will experience frustration and demotivation. The rest of the company may be exposed to harmful consequences.
- **Too little freedom: Captive.** If the team is given less freedom than matches their maturity, they will feel captive or imprisoned by their environment. They lack the room for initiative; they will just follow orders, and they will be unable to grow as a team and develop their own working methods. As a consequence, they will also experience frustration and demotivation, which may affect the quality of the product or service they deliver and the satisfaction of the customers of those products or services.

Good Zone

The good zone is located in the middle, the area where maturity and freedom are in balance, providing the team with clarity, boundaries, and room for their own input. These are the ideal conditions in which the team can take ownership. Ownership isn't dependent on maturity. In fact, ownership can still take place even when team maturity is low if the team has the appropriate level of freedom; all they need is just a little more freedom than their current maturity.

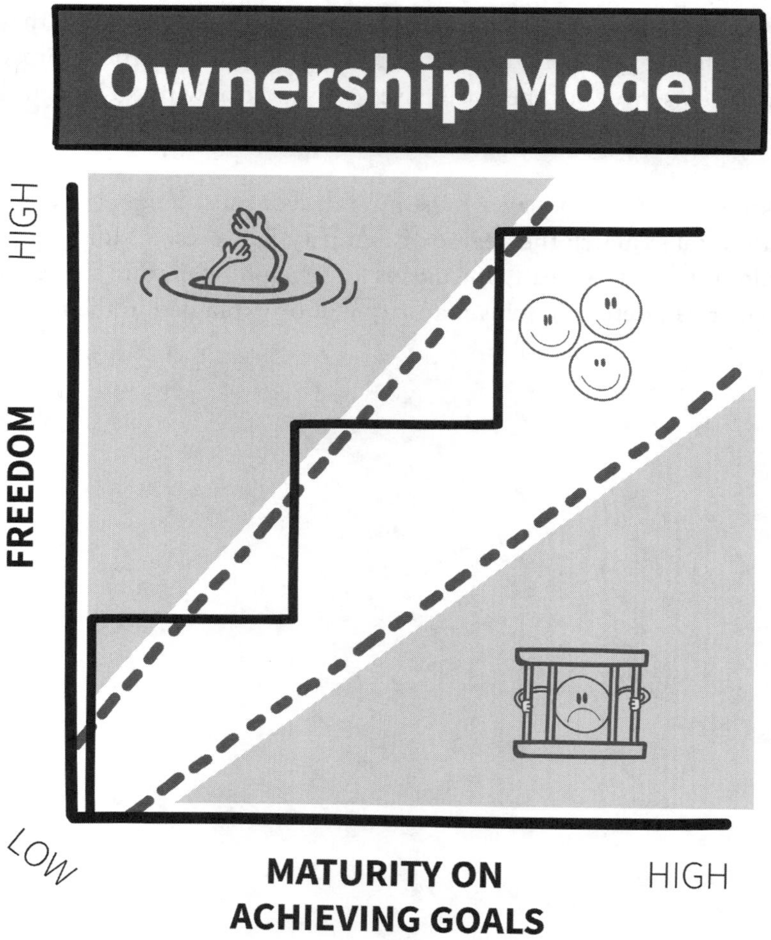

Figure 2.2 Ownership Model with staircase

Staircase

A staircase can be added to the Ownership Model (see Figure 2.2). The staircase in the good zone visualizes the growth of the team. The team gets more freedom so that team members can grow in maturity. Then they get more freedom again so they can grow further. That is why the staircase first goes up, then to the right and then back up again. The staircase walks on the edge of the chaos zone. This is really important. Teams will get more freedom than they can currently handle, but that's crucial for them to learn as they go. For example, they can manage the stakeholders themselves, but they still have to learn how to properly do that. Or they can prioritize the improvement topics themselves, but they still have to discover how to do that in the best manner.

To know when the manager must intervene or must let go, the degree of freedom must match the degree of maturity; however, deciding how much freedom the team is ready for means knowing how mature the team is. How a manager can determine this maturity will be explained in the next section.

2.3 HOW MATURE IS MY TEAM?

A leader doesn't need to be needed.

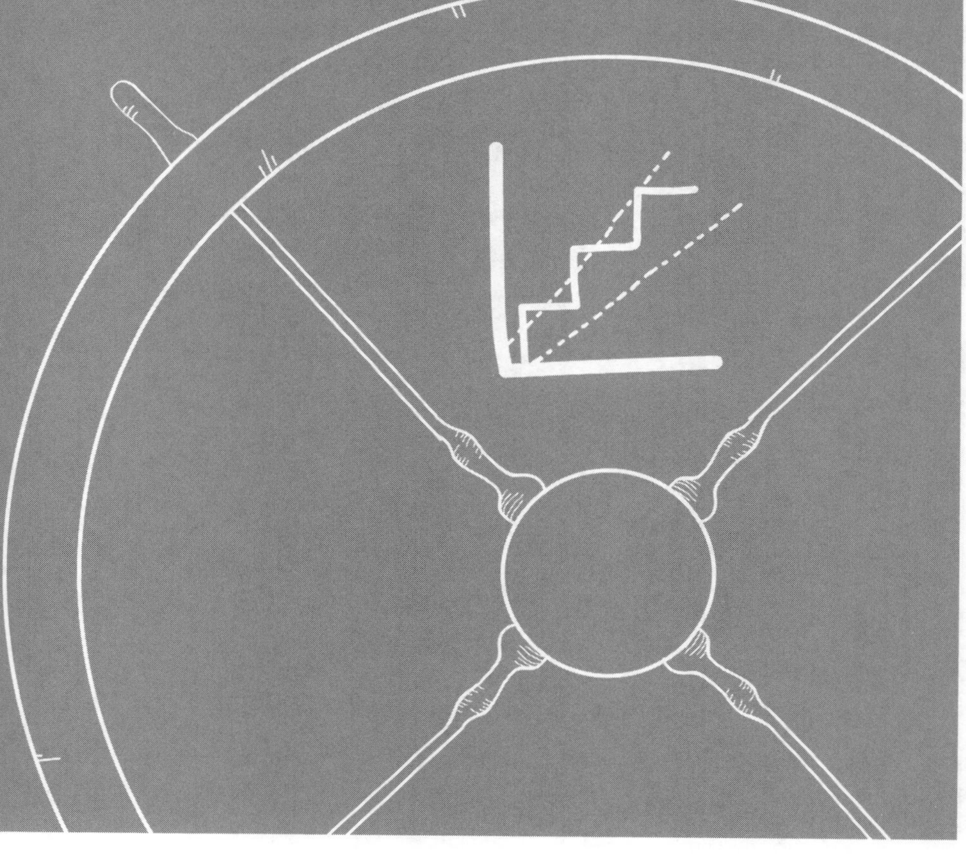

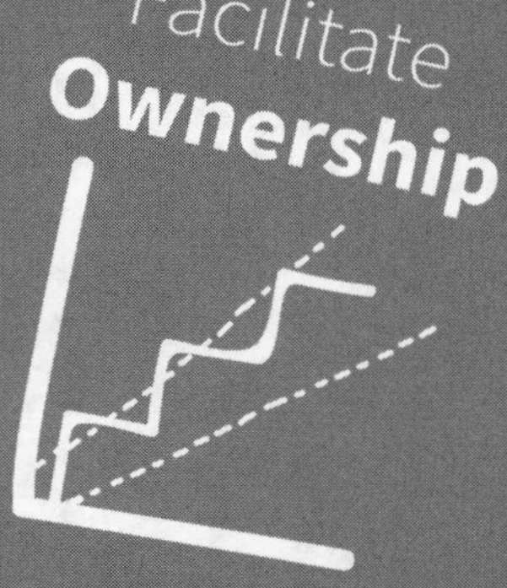

Introduction Questions

1. Which of your teams are high in maturity?
2. Do you and your teams have the same tangible expectations of high maturity?

The purpose of knowing the maturity level of a team isn't to compare or judge the teams. Maturity does not describe whether one team is better than another. Rather, it is a snapshot in time to help everyone understand what can be expected from a given team. Again, the purpose of knowing the maturity level is to align the freedom and autonomy of the team accordingly to drive ownership. Or even better, it is to give them the freedom and autonomy they need to grow further. This truly drives ownership. Ownership is crucial for self-managing teams. It makes them proactive, acting like local entrepreneurs to make the products and services better.

The maturity of teams becomes clear because the model indicates, for each step of the staircase, what they want to achieve. When the teams and the agile leader work together to make the staircase clear, the overall expectations align. With this, the maturity of the team is cut up into stages. Subsequently, it can be indicated per stage what a team can achieve in order to demonstrably have this degree of mastery. This makes the maturity of teams much more measurable. Also, the expectations of the stakeholders, the other teams, and the agile leader are aligned.

Stages in Maturity

The stages of maturity should be chosen to avoid making comparisons or judgments between teams. The stages of maturity can be named in different ways (see Figure 2.3). Teams can get the following:

- A name or label, for example, "junior" or "senior"
- A number of stars, as in a 0-, 1-, 2-, or 3-star team
- A name like "cottage," "villa," and "skyscraper"
- A number like "base camp," "camp 1," "camp 2," …, and "summit"

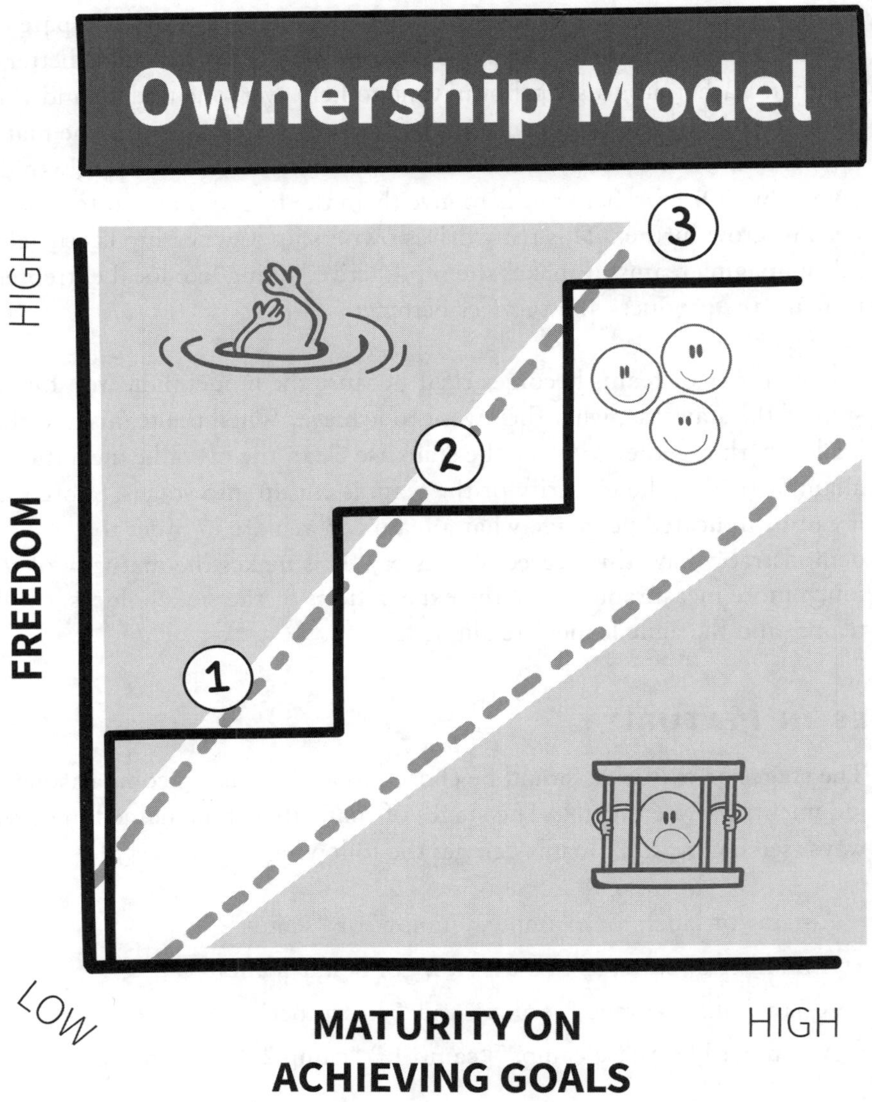

Figure 2.3 Stages in maturity in the Ownership Model

Together with the teams, the agile leader defines what each team must achieve to reach the next stage; if the achievements are not measurable, differences in interpretation will cause ownership to disappear. But you can't define *how* the teams will achieve their goals or ownership will also disappear. It must also be clear what the teams must achieve without prescribing how they do it. You want them to work *smarter* and *achieve* more, not necessarily to work *harder* and *do* more. As with a sports team, the maturity is measured by what they achieve in their competition—how many matches they win—not by their successful passes or percentage of ball possessions. When they are champions in their current level of competition, they move to the next higher level of play. If they are really great, they will win the equivalent of the league championship.

Different organizations can work with different Ownership Models. For example, software development teams can demonstrate their maturity as follows. Every two weeks the satisfaction level of three groups is measured: the team itself, the product owner, and the most important stakeholder of the team. If the team then gets at least a 7 out of all three groups in three consecutive sprints, they can become a 1-star team. A 2-star team gets structurally higher satisfaction: a 7.5. And a 3-star team gets an 8 or higher. In addition, extra conditions are added for 2- and 3-star teams. A 2-star team must know and maintain its KVI (see Part 1, "Co-Create Goals"). A 3-star team must show growth in the KVI and also be able to automatically release to customers every day.

Other Indicators

Besides satisfaction, other indicators can also be used to make the mastery tangible. Examples are margin per team member, the number of new large customers per quarter, and the sales conversion figures. Another example is the number of manual actions per 1,000 customers—the fewer manual actions, the more scalable the team.

It is often difficult in practice to properly cut the maturity of a team into stages. For this, it is useful to know what recognizable stages of maturity are. In the next section, I explain how most teams grow.

2.4 HOW DO TYPICAL TEAMS GROW?

The courage of leadership is giving others the chance to succeed even though you bear the responsibility if they fail.

– Simon Sinek

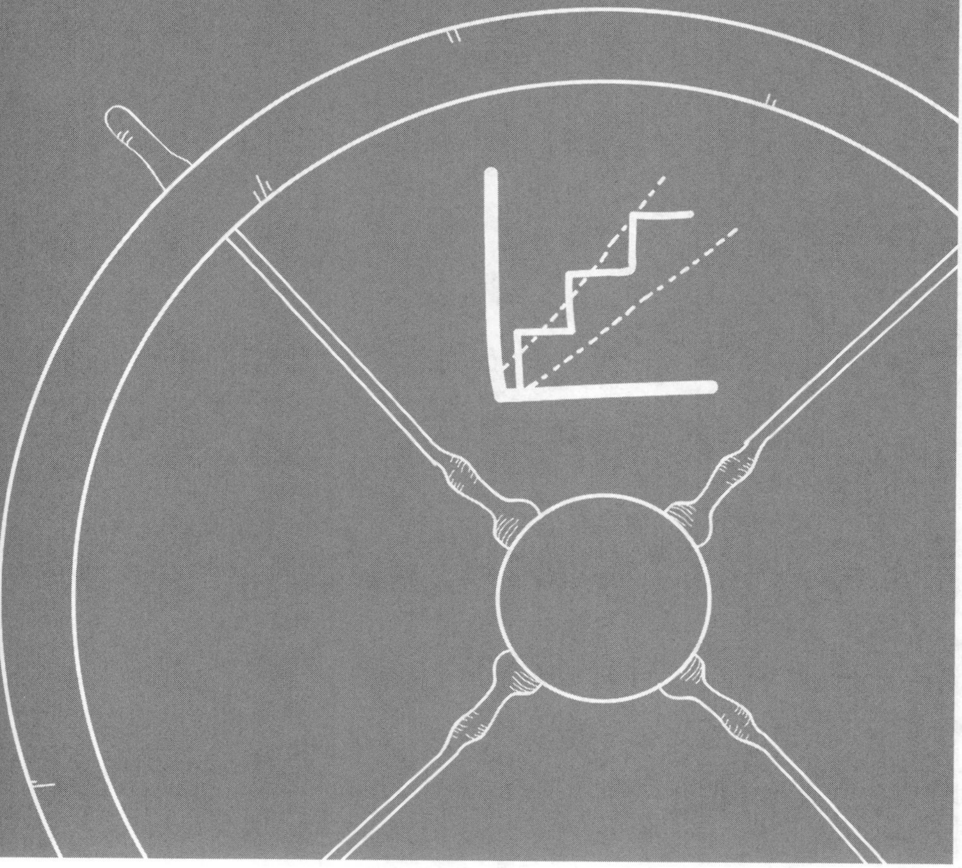

Introduction Questions

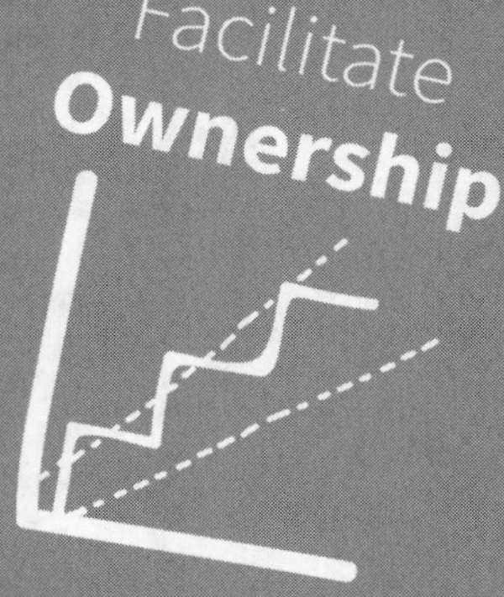

1. What do you prefer—to design the right environment for the teams, or to actively be part of a team?
2. Do you have the patience it takes to let a team grow?

Over the past years, I've seen multiple teams grow. I noticed that many teams go through almost the same stages of maturity. These stages are shown in Table 2.1.

Table 2.1 Stages of maturity

#	Stage	Description
0	Start	Collaboration emerges.
1	Output	The team gives reliable forecasts, manages their stakeholders, and often delivers what they promised.
2	Quality	The team increases their craftsmanship and mastery. They use this to deliver high quality.
3	Scaling	The team collaborates intensively with other teams and fosters synergy over multiple teams.
4	Impact	Multiple teams work smarter. They collaborate on creating a higher customer impact. They become the trusted advisors of their customers.

Successful agile leaders adjust their own behavior to match the stage of maturity of their team. It is important that a leader recognizes how teams grow. The following, therefore, is an explanation of the different stages.

Stage 0, Start

In the start-up stage, the team focuses on building cooperation between members. They are busy getting to know each other and the environment and learning to work well together. The role of the agile leader in this stage is simply to manage. Teams grow faster in this stage when they have a leader who helps them arrange and coordinate things. The team needs clarity and transparency about work backlogs, team agreements, short-term objectives, work instructions, and holiday plans. If the agile leader takes care of this, the right environment for the team emerges to let the team negotiate their agreements, build trust, and gain experience. The team is usually not yet mature enough to manage its own priorities towards the stakeholders, so it helps if the agile leader creates clarity about who determines the priorities and what the overall priorities are. He can then coach the team to manage the expectations and satisfaction of stakeholders. At the same time, the agile leader coaches the team to become increasingly independent when they are planning activities and giving each other honest feedback.

STAGE 1, OUTPUT

To reach the first stage of maturity, output, the team has shown that they can plan their own work, they are able to manage stakeholder expectations effectively, and they are able to meet those expectations with healthy reliability. To achieve this, team members know each other's competencies, they have a realistic understanding of what they can reasonably accomplish, and they hold each other accountable on the agreements made. They also give feedback to each other regarding everyone's contribution to the result, each other's attitudes and behavior, and their mutual competencies. They also have a clear understanding of the impact they want to deliver to the customer.

With greater team independence, the agile leader is increasingly becoming the facilitator of the team at this stage. He makes fewer and fewer choices for the team, instead guiding them to make their own choices. He shares his experience and insight and stimulates the team to develop their knowledge and skills. In addition, the leader guides the clarification of the customer impact and the associated KVI (see Part 1). He is officially still managing them, but he encourages them to make their own decisions and gives them the freedom and permission to make mistakes and learn from the experience. This extends to giving them permission to question and challenge the opinions of the agile leader, to discuss matters as peers, to offer reasoned resistance, and to think and act critically.

STAGE 2, QUALITY

To reach the second stage of maturity, the team has demonstrated that they are continuously improving the quality of their work. Team members have developed insight into their talents and craftsmanship, and they give each other feedback on the quality and maturity of their skills. They share knowledge or enroll in training and education to increase their skills. The agile leader has become mostly a facilitator; he hardly needs to say anything, he sometimes lacks the knowledge and experience that team members have to guide the team in growing their quality, and he becomes more detached from the daily work of the team.

Stage 3, Scaling

To reach the third stage of maturity, scaling, the team has demonstrated that they are able to cooperate, align, and build synergy with other teams. They mentor, coach, and guide other teams to grow their own maturity. At the same time, they are open to learning from and being coached by other teams. Together, the teams grow their craftsmanship, innovation, and quality. They work in a constructive atmosphere of fun, cooperation, honesty, and knowledge sharing between teams. The teams stimulate each other in the development of their talents and also hold other teams accountable on agreements and promises made.

The agile leader is now wholly focused on the collaborative environment. He inspires, motivates, and rewards teams when they collaborate. He removes impediments that block synergy and effectiveness. The agile leader is no longer needed for the daily work. He empowers the teams to learn faster from customers (see Part 3, "Learn Faster") and increase the customer impact.

Stage 4, Impact

To reach the fourth stage of maturity, impact, several teams will have demonstrated that they are working well together and continuously improving. Their joint decisions are good, and they have implemented improvements and tested innovative ideas with customers. They show that they have such a level of craftsmanship that they say no to work that does not contribute (enough) to a higher customer impact. They receive quick feedback from customers on what they have done (see Part 3). This enables them to continuously work smarter. The agile leader now shifts completely, almost to the role of a servant. There is hardly any hierarchy anymore, and the leader actually only steers the culture (see Part 4, "Design Healthy Habits"). He inspires the team to continue to grow, to continue to challenge themselves, and to push boundaries.

AFTER THAT?

After stage 4 comes teams that perform beyond market standards. Marketing, sales, support, and development teams work closely and mature together. In synergy, they achieve beyond market standards. They act as a small company within a larger company. These teams take ownership of the entire company as real entrepreneurs: from market proposition to price strategy and from sales to support.

2.5 HOW CAN THE BORDERS BE ALIGNED WITH THE MATURITY?

Because we all agreed to drive on the right side of the road (as in, not on the wrong side of the road 😉), stop for a red light, and respect the speed limit, we actually increase the freedom and autonomy!

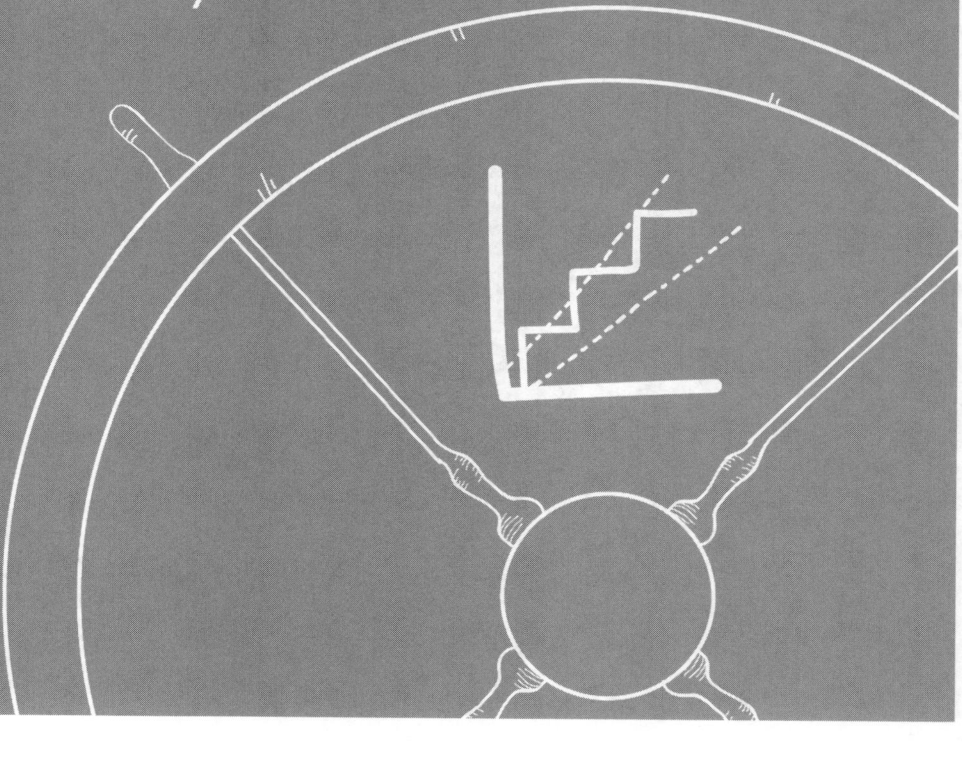

Introduction Questions

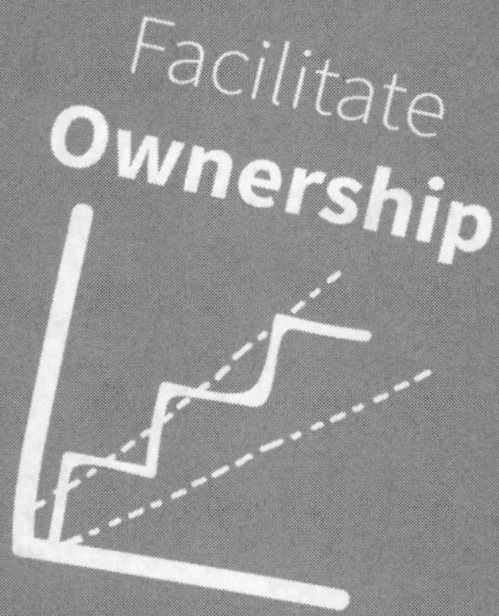

1. How much freedom can highly mature teams get from you in the end?
2. Which borders are needed to increase the freedom and autonomy in your teams?

Mature teams need broader and fewer borders than teams who are just starting. To maximize ownership in teams, the agile leader must allow the borders to expand with maturity. But what are the right borders? What are concrete examples of broader freedom? Are there such mature teams that they have complete and total freedom? Or do self-managing teams still need borders?

Concretely Expanding the Borders

By expanding the borders in steps, the agile leader creates clarity for the team. It is important that the borders remain clear and that the steps are transparent, so there must be several steps between zero freedom, whereby the agile leader prescribes matters, to complete freedom, whereby the team can independently determine and regulate everything. A first step might be that the team brainstorms with the manager but that the manager still makes the decision; the next step might be for the team and the manager to come to a decision together; a further step might be that the team itself makes a decision after the supervisor has been consulted; a final step might be that the team does not even have to inform the manager about the choice. This is a concrete and practical approach to gradually broaden the borders.

Freedom is different for each topic or theme. There are topics in which even a starting team is given a lot of freedom and others where even a high-maturity team has little freedom. For example, a starting team can often arrange their own holiday planning and a high-maturity team cannot give themselves an unlimited salary increase. For topics such as improvement budgets, team composition, and assessment, clear borders are required that grow with maturity. In practice, it is often difficult to determine freedom for these kinds of themes. This is because, on one hand, a topic must be split into subjects, and on the other, the expectations of freedom differ from person to person. Precisely for this reason, the fourth tool of the toolkit has been developed: the Freedom

Matrix. I will first explain how themes can be split and then I will explain the Freedom Matrix.

THEME EXAMPLE 1: TEAM COMPOSITION

Freedom around the theme "team composition" is difficult to make concrete because it consists of various topics. For example, there is the hiring of team members on the basis of a vacancy, changing team members between two or more teams, contracting an external employee, and dismissing an employee. The freedom on each of these facets has to be determined for each stage of maturity. For example, a starting team can probably change team members but can't yet autonomously hire new members based on a vacancy. The team only gets this freedom when they are more mature. The question is whether it is wise to give a highly mature team the freedom to fire a colleague.

THEME EXAMPLE 2: RATING

The freedom surrounding the evaluation and assessment of employees also consists of several subjects—for example, informal feedback, a positive evaluation, a negative evaluation with consequences, and the determination of the bonus split or salary increase. It's wise to make the freedom for each stage of maturity on each of these topics concrete. It is good when a starting team immediately learns to give each other feedback. Some highly mature teams determine—given a fixed budget—the distribution of the bonus and the salary increase among themselves.

TOOL 4: FREEDOM MATRIX

Boundaries must be tangible, and freedom must gradually increase as team maturity increases. A tool that helps with this is the Freedom Matrix. This tool is based on the Delegation Board from Management 3.0, developed by Jurgen Appelo.[2] The Freedom Matrix makes the connection between the maturity of the team and the freedom the team receives on specific topics. By doing this, this fourth tool of the agile leadership toolkit makes it clear which freedoms the team gets when. As a result, expectations about freedom become explicit and can be discussed and improved. The Freedom Matrix looks like Figure 2.4.

2. https://management30.com/practice/delegation-poker/

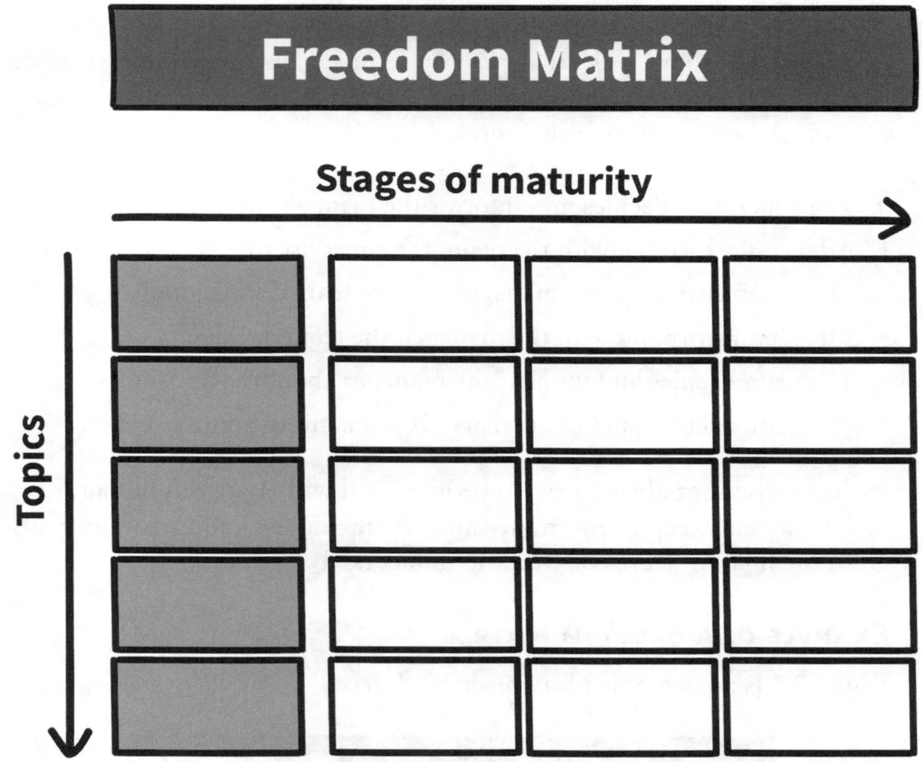

Figure 2.4 The Freedom Matrix

Horizontal Axis: Stages of Maturity

As mentioned, the stages of maturity could be designated as junior, medium, and senior teams, or 1-, 2-, and 3-star teams.

Vertical Axis: Topics

A separate row is used for each of the concrete subjects. These can be topics as mentioned earlier: changing team members between teams, giving informal feedback, or releasing an external employee.

CELLS: FREEDOMS

In the cells, freedom is clearly stated on a subject at a given stage of maturity. This freedom has been split into steps or levels. This way, teams can gradually gain more freedom during their growth.

0. The supervisor decides and informs the team about this.
1. After brainstorming with the team, the supervisor makes the decision.
2. After brainstorming, the manager and the team decide jointly.
3. After brainstorming with the manager, the team decides.
4. The team decides and informs the manager about the decision.
5. The team decides, and the manager is not actively informed.

Freedom does not always have to be increased with a growth in maturity; it may be wise to keep freedom the same. A starting or junior team may also be given the highest degree of freedom immediately.

EXAMPLE OF A FREEDOM MATRIX

Figure 2.5 is an example of a Freedom Matrix.

Freedom Matrix

	Junior	Medium	Senior
Interviews	3	4	5
$2k invest	3	4	4
Firing	0	1	1
Divide Bonus	0	2	4

Figure 2.5 Example Freedom Matrix

In this example, a Junior team gets freedom 3 for handling the interviews for new team members. This means that they have to consult their manager and ask his advice prior to making a decision. A Medium team can interview, filter, and choose new team members based on a vacancy themselves. They only have to keep their leader informed of the final decision.

Next, they get a quarterly $2,000 investment budget. A Junior team still has to ask the manager for advice prior to spending the budget. Medium and Senior teams only have to inform their manager on how they spent it.

Firing of team members is still done by the manager. For a Junior team, the manager just tells why he has fired a person. For more mature teams, the manager brainstorms or consults with the team prior to making the decision.

In this example, the team gets a quarterly bonus. For a Junior team, the manager divides the bonus. But a Senior team can decide themselves on how to divide the bonus. The manager only tells the team the amount of bonus they can divide among themselves.

2.6 WHEN DOES THE OWNERSHIP MODEL WORK AND WHEN DOES IT NOT?

I have a definition of success. For me, it's very simple. It's not about wealth and fame and power. It's about how many shining eyes I have around me.

– Benjamin Zander, conductor and musical director of the Boston Philharmonic Orchestra

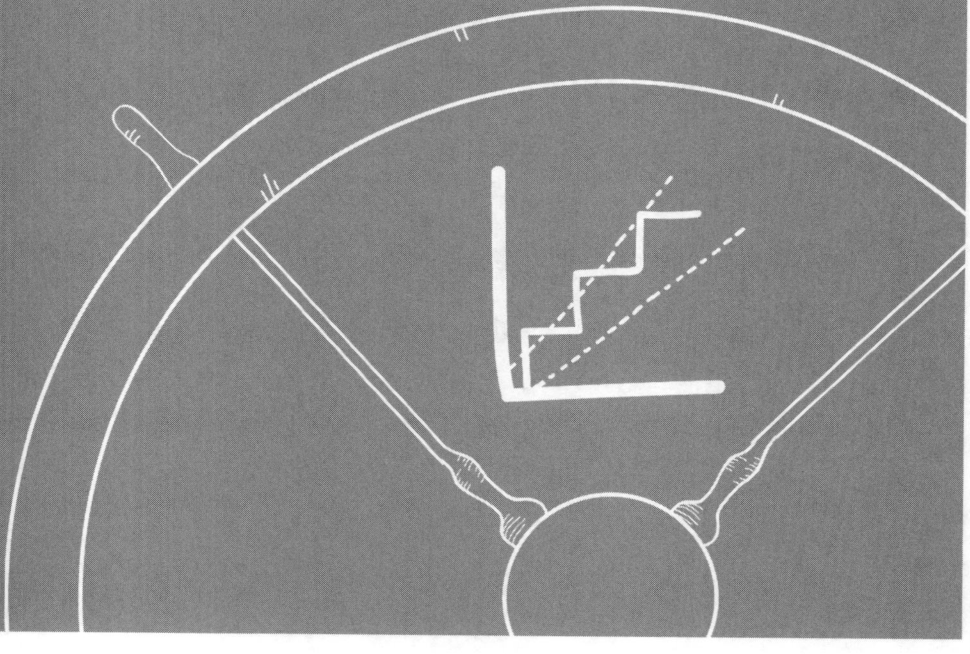

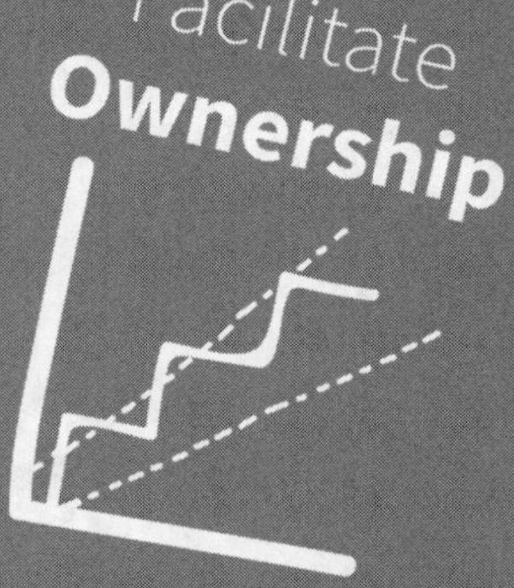

Introduction Questions

1. What makes your team interested in becoming more mature? What do they get in return?
2. Which employees dare to give you honest and strong personal feedback?

The Ownership Model requires some conditions to be satisfied in order to work.

Teams Need a Single Concrete, Shared Goal

A team can only self-organize if it is clear what they have to achieve. Without a concrete and shared goal, team members will perform their own work; the team ceases to function as a team. They fail to take on ownership, and the value delivered to customers suffers.

A KVI provides the team with a concrete and shared goal that supersedes individual goals. A single, concrete, shared goal helps the team come together to achieve the shared goal. In short, it helps them achieve ownership. As they continue to grow, they need lower and wider boundaries from their leader.

Teams Should Be Able to Give Open Feedback to the Leader to Maintain Ownership

Teams must be able to be transparent about how things are going, about what gives them energy, and about what frustrates them. Without open feedback, including feedback about how the agile leader is doing and feedback to each other, the team will become reactive; they will exhibit distrust, and they will hold back on their feedback. This kind of environment kills ownership. To create a culture of open feedback, trust, and learning, effective agile leaders have to set the right example. They need to make themselves open to feedback, even critical feedback. They need to be open about their own mistakes and shortcomings and ask for help from the team to grow continuously. They indicate what they are good at but also where they lack talents or skills. They talk about their own mistakes in a vulnerable and often humorous manner, and by doing so they make it safe for the rest of the team to do the same. This is the start of the kind of culture that allows ownership to flourish.

Teams Need to Focus on Working Smarter

Working harder doesn't scale; if teams have to work harder to get better results, they will lack the time to learn and grow as a team. Highly mature teams make smart use of software to partially or fully automate their delivery processes. Doing so enables them to grow their customer impact while leaving time to continuously improve. Effective leaders value teams based on what achieve, not on what they do. For example, a team's goal should be to increase customer satisfaction, increase use by the customer, or increase profit margin, not to increase the number of customer calls, the number of deliveries, or the number of new features shipped.

Quick Customer Appreciation

Users who are constantly very satisfied with what the teams do for them are likely to be served by a highly mature team. If the team receives feedback quickly and regularly from customers, they also gain quick insight into what they can improve. Agile leaders need to help teams shorten the learning loop with the customer (see Part 3). For example, if it takes 12 months to receive feedback on what they are doing today, giving teams more freedom is almost impossible (and has little value) because it's virtually impossible to assess their maturity.

Agile Leaders Need to Escape the Yearly Employee Feedback Ritual

When agile leaders start using the Ownership Model, they are often trapped in ritualistic annual feedback and appraisal cycles. In the time gap between events and feedback, opportunities for improvement are lost. Feedback and assessment must be continuous to enable continuous improvement.

Resilience

Often, when leaders start using the Ownership Model, there is initially a lot of attention and focus on it. But too often this focus diminishes over time. Effective agile leaders show resilience and maintain this focus for several years in a row. It can take a lot of time to grow and nurture the teams and continuously improve the environment; this isn't achieved in a few months. For agile leaders, the most important focus regarding their teams should be whether they are still in ownership. They continuously ask, "What can I do to improve your environment?" And this should not occur for the first months only; rather, agile leaders keep bringing that resilience.

Summary of Part 2—Facilitate Ownership

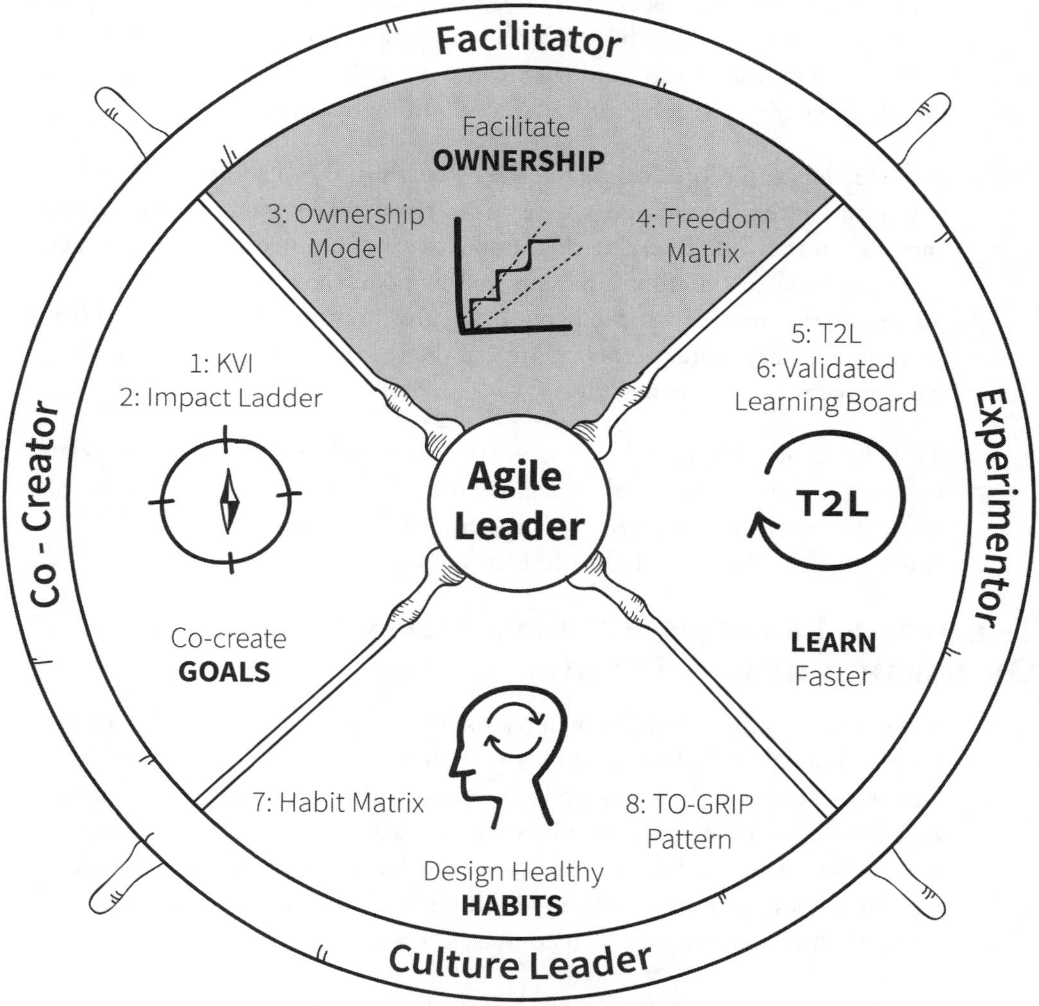

In this second part of the steering wheel, we look at how the leader can facilitate ownership. See the figure above for the visualization of Part 2. Self-managing teams need ownership to achieve their ambitions and objectives. Ownership is actually present when teams feel responsible and accountable for the results of their products and services. Teams that take on ownership are different from average teams; they are proactive and have both the passion and the energy to make an impact for customers. They work together, give each other feedback, are open-minded, and learn continuously. They also help other teams to grow. They also take ownership of both the strategy and its implementation. They have the deep understanding that they own their own challenges, solutions, and customers. This gives the teams pride, creativity, energy, passion, and satisfaction in their work.

Agile leaders can't force teams to take ownership; they can only create an environment that encourages the teams to freely take ownership and supports them when they do. To create this supportive environment, the agile leader must intervene at the right moments and let go at the right moments, as guided by the maturity of the team. If the freedom the team is granted from their agile leader matches their maturity, the team will be given the right environment to take ownership.

The Ownership Model helps to make the relationship between maturity and freedom tangible. The Freedom Matrix provides a way to make freedom and maturity visible and concrete, by subject. See Figure 2.6 and Figure 2.7, respectively, for larger visualizations of these tools.

The Agile Leader's Responsibility to Facilitate Ownership in His Team(s)

When the work is complex, when teams have to grow continuously, and when the team members have to find creative solutions every day to really help customers, they need ownership to be successful. Ownership enables them to be creative and develop innovative solutions that benefit customers. These teams don't wait for others come up with solutions and do not blame the circumstances; they are constantly looking for better solutions and new opportunities to better serve customers.

The agile leader's most important responsibility is to facilitate an environment in which the teams can take ownership and, in doing so, to continuously improve as a facilitator. By doing so, he becomes increasingly skilled in the following:

- **Asking powerful questions of the team.** Powerful questions increase creativity, promote honesty and transparency, stimulate out-of-the-box thinking, and focus on the outcome. By asking powerful questions, the teams are invited to take action, discover solutions, and make things clear and explicit.

- **Self-reflection.** The behavior of the teams is a mirror of the environment we agile leaders create. Nobody comes to his or her work thinking, "Today I want to be demotivated, criticize others, and distrust my boss." When people don't have that spark in their eye called ownership, it's not because they want it to be that way. It's because we agile leaders haven't yet improved the environment enough. Being a better facilitator of ownership goes hand-in-hand with being better at reflecting on one's own behavior.
- **Team process.** Good teams reflect, modify, and amplify each other's ideas into even better ideas, seeking synergies to produce a better result. Together they are smarter than the sum of team members' parts. Building these awesome teams is a difficult but crucial skill to master.
- **Growth of craftsmanship among team members.** People in the successful agile teams are multiskilled, which means they master different areas of expertise. They need an environment that not only promotes knowledge transfer and skill development but also inspires them to become true craftsmen at several areas of expertise.

Tangible Actions

The following are some tangible actions to put the tools, examples, and ideas from Part 2 into practice.

1. **Make explicit what you expect from high maturity teams.** Share your vision of awesome and pinnacle teams. Make this as concrete and as stretching as possible.
2. **Ask for concrete changes in freedom.** Allow yourself to be surprised. Often the need for freedom of the team itself is different from what the agile leader expects.
3. **Make your expectations about the growth of the teams concrete.** Which stage in maturity do you expect the teams to go through in the coming six months? Help them reflect on what they will need from themselves, and from you, to get there.
4. **Make team maturity deltas a focus of the team retrospectives.** In addition to improving how the team works, make focus on the evolving maturity of the team one of the most important parts of team retrospectives.

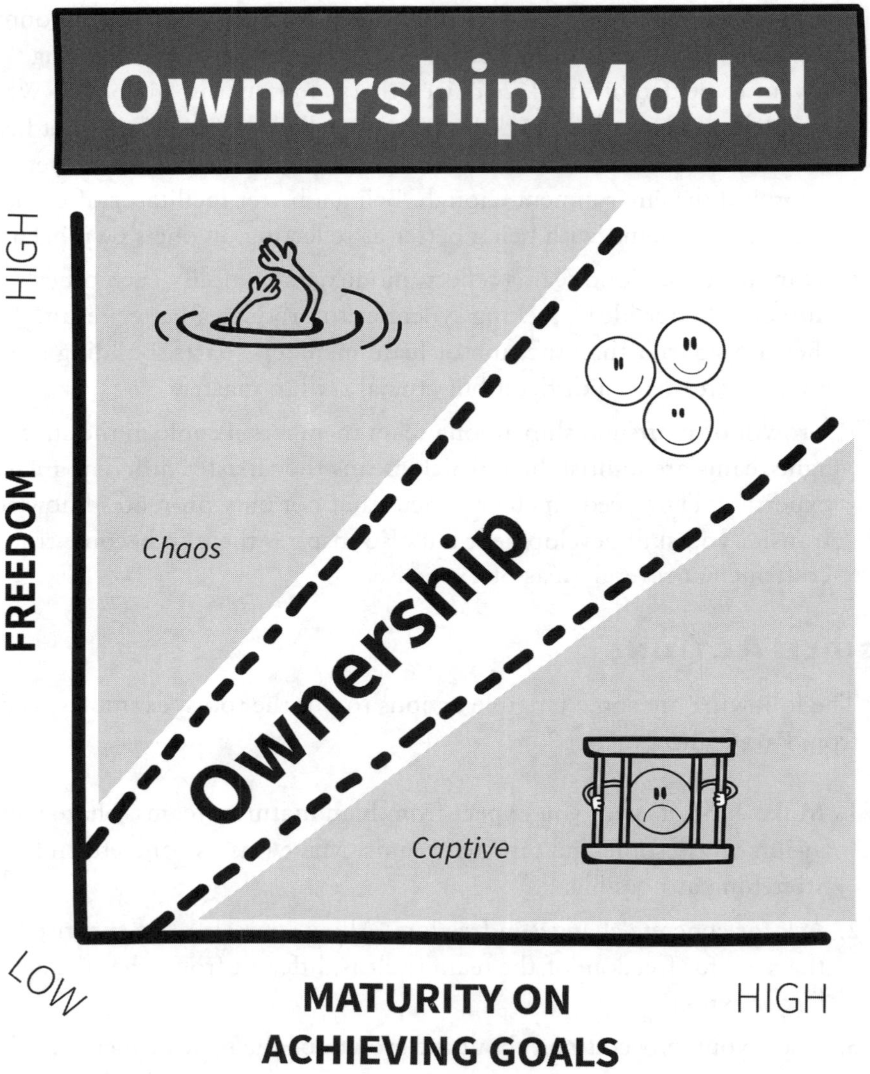

Figure 2.6 Large Ownership Model

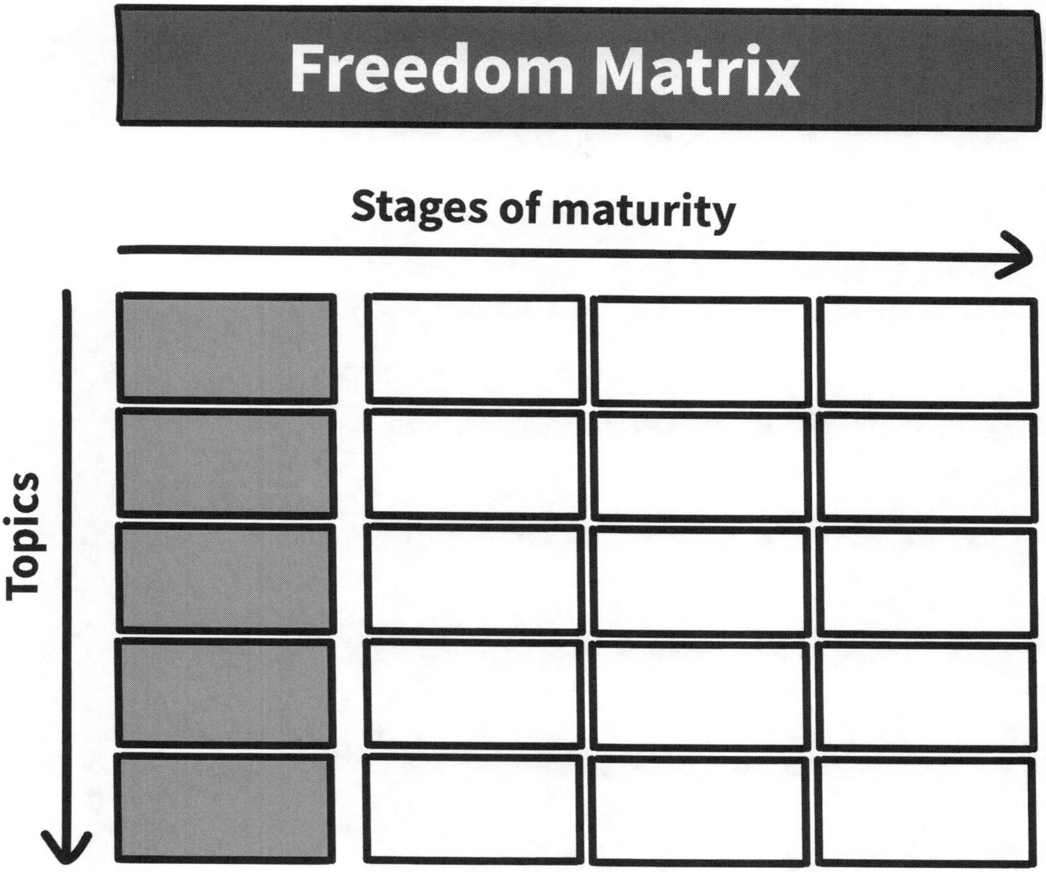

Figure 2.7 Large Freedom Matrix

Notes

PART 3
Learn Faster

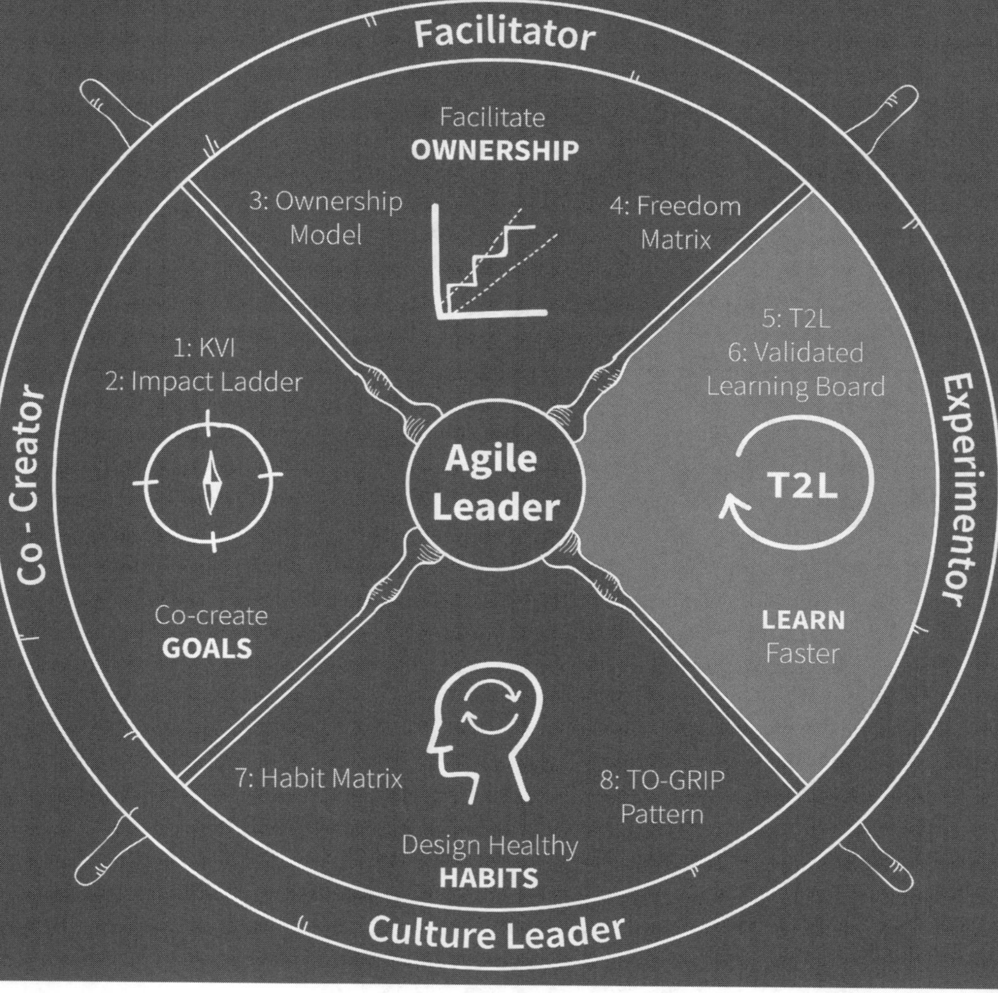

3.1 HOW DO YOU KNOW YOUR TEAMS ARE DOING THE RIGHT THINGS?

Only by preparing the meal and tasting it can one discover whether a recipe is a good recipe.

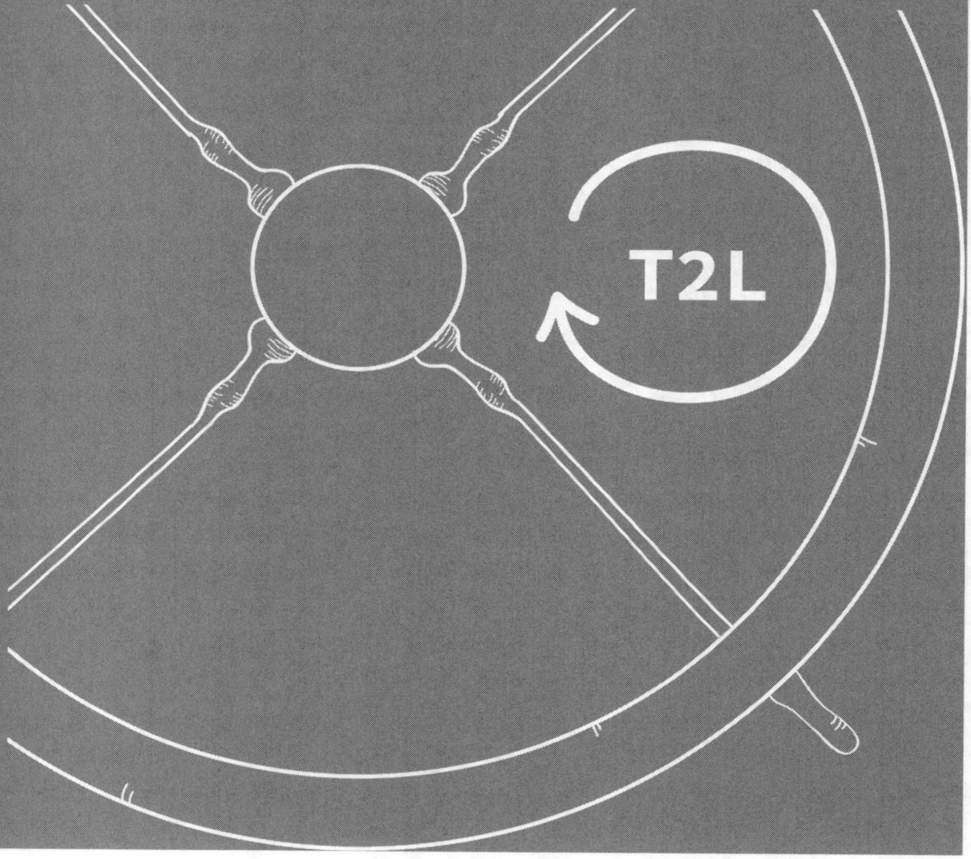

Introduction Questions

1. What is your proof that your teams are doing the right thing?
2. When will teams receive customer feedback on their choices of today?

T2L LEARN Faster

Introduction Story

Around 2005 I started my agile journey as a brand new agile leader by building a great innovative new product: Revent. The old product had existed for more than ten years and was the market leader, but it was threatened to be overtaken by the competition. New functionalities were difficult to add, and the method of working was outdated. We wanted to make something revolutionary to remain market leader; that is why the director made the firm decision to invest in a new product right away. We fortunately got all the space in the world from him. We had good ideas and were convinced that this new product would easily beat the competition, not only in the Netherlands but also abroad. In retrospect, I think, if only we had dealt with it differently, then we would not have had such a huge problem two years later.

I was excited and full of enthusiasm. We had created a new product using new techniques and a new methodology. We used Scrum as a method and worked with sprints of two weeks, which meant that every two weeks we had a new demo version (an "increment" within Scrum), which we showed to all sorts of stakeholders. They were very satisfied. After a few months we even went to the customer with the product for a demo of the new functionality. We were very proud that—thanks to Scrum—we were already able to give a demo. The first customers were enthusiastic and indicated that they were more than willing to buy the new product soon. They were impressed by our smart algorithms that could automatically handle all kinds of situations.

In addition, we kept a nice schedule for the project, we held steering-committee meetings with the director, and all known KPIs were green. We even received test scenarios from customers that we used to test the new product continually. To further improve the good cooperation in the team, we held interim evaluation moments ("retrospectives" within Scrum). After more than two years of intensive development, testing, and processing of feedback, we worked toward the first release. It was a nice phase in which we still worked together with a lot of energy. As a team, we thought it would be nice to show our baby to the outside world. A select group of customers now really started working with the release. It was not until then that some aspect of the big underlying problem became visible to me. In the end, it took us more than a year to really make the new product work.

After the first release came the big disappointment. We noticed that customers did not switch to the new product even though, in many areas, it worked a good deal better than the old one. We had built smart algorithms that would make life easier for users. However, there were many exceptional situations that the new product could not handle. This was such a blockade for our customers that they had to fall back on the old (existing) product.

What had we overlooked? What were we forgetting? We thought we were processing customer feedback well, but we had made a crucial mistake. We received feedback from customers on our own organized demos. But that was feedback on a laboratory situation, in a defined context in which the new product worked fantastically. At that moment we did not have any feedback of real use. These customers were users of the current product, but not yet of the new product with the new functionalities. So, our crucial mistake was that we were going to make a version that really worked too late. We should have made sure that within a few months we already had a version that customers could really use. Then we would have received feedback from real users rather than an opinion during a demo. With this feedback, through the use of real customers, as an agile leader I could have really known whether we were working on the right things as a team, such as whether we took into account enough exceptions; whether the product really benefited users in practice; and whether the performance, stability, and quality were sufficient.

My conclusion is that if we had processed the feedback from real users at an early stage, we could have made adjustments much earlier. And we would have had a better product sooner that would improve sales much more quickly. After three years, we probably would have had many happy customers.

Control Over Activities

If after a while it appears that products from a team are not sold, are unreliable, or require a lot of maintenance, the agile leader remains responsible for this. Does his team ensure that thousands of customers can visit the website at the same time? Do the reports produced contain the correct figures and information? Does his sales team not promise too many golden mountains in the sales process? The agile leader wants to know if the team members are performing their work well. Ideally, he ensures that the team receives immediate insight on this so that the team can make adjustments themselves. But he doesn't want to micromanage the team, get detailed updates, and double-check the most important risks. On the other hand, he also doesn't want to blindly trust the teams for years without any updates or information. But how does he find the balance between these two unwanted extremes? How can he have control over the activities without micromanaging on a daily basis and without blindly trusting for years without insight?

The solution lies in fast feedback from actual users. This is the *learning loop*: the process of retrieving user feedback and learning from it. The agile leader has to create an environment in which teams get quick feedback from actual users and can spend time on learning from this feedback. Agile teams then can optimize their learning loop. I will explain what this learning loop is exactly and how teams can adjust it.

> *An agile leader inspires and supports his teams to continuously learn from the feedback from real users.*

ING is a bank founded in the Netherlands. This company developed an app that makes it easy to transfer money. With the first version, ING's customers could only view their balance. ING then made small improvements in the app, and new functionalities were added. By listening to the feedback from users, ING was better able to determine the needs of the users and how they could better connect to them. As a result, other and better choices were made about the functionalities of the banking app. Today users can look up credits and debits, create savings accounts, and issue payment requests. The agile approach thus resulted in an app that many customers use every day to their full satisfaction.

At the start, YouTube was primarily intended as a dating site where the user could create his own TV (tube) in order to find his future partner. By processing customer feedback, the vision of the site has changed and is now being used for all types of videos.

At the creation of Twitter, codes such as #hashtag and @at were not yet known at all. These actually arose spontaneously because a few customers started using them. Twitter used this feedback to innovate and built, among other things, search functionalities and trends around it. The founder of Twitter, Evan Williams, found the use of this kind of code too nerdy and that is why he didn't use them. But by responding to real customer use, the codes are now commonly used on Twitter and other social media.

> *The most important piece of information when trying to determine whether teams are doing the right thing is frequent feedback from actual users.*

So instead of getting all kinds of detailed reports, spending time double-checking risks, and asking questions on the forecast, the agile leader is often more effective when he spends time optimizing the learning loop. This is because the most important piece of information when trying to determine whether teams are doing the right thing is frequent feedback from actual users. But what is a good learning loop? How should "frequent" be defined? And how can the agile leader optimize this learning loop? I will answer these questions in the next paragraphs and sections.

What Is the Learning Loop?

The cyclic process of retrieving feedback from users, learning from them, and implementing improvements in the product is called the *learning loop*. The learning loop is a means for the team members to know whether they are doing the right work. They can quickly adjust themselves based on new insights. By applying the learning loop, the team becomes more self-organizing and more agile. The learning loop is shown in Figure 3.1.

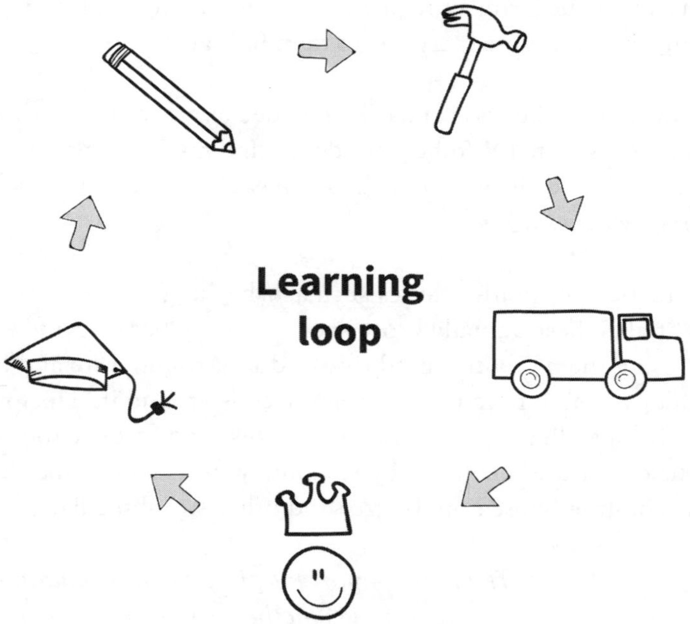

Figure 3.1 The learning loop

During the learning loop, the team goes through the following five steps:

1. **Sketch.** In this first step, team, stakeholders, and customers together think about all kinds of ideas to expand a product or service. The most important ideas are elaborated in a sketch: a drawing, illustration, or description. "Sketch" means that not everything needs to be worked out in detail, which happens during the next steps. Sketching increases creativity, leaving room for refreshing solutions.

2. **Build.** In the next step, build, the team gets to work with the most important ideas and actually incorporates these into a product or service. The team elaborates on the details of the ideas in consultation with stakeholders and customers. In the meantime, the team gives demos of the product to stakeholders and customers for the following reasons:
   a. To discuss whether the details have been processed correctly
   b. To brainstorm further details
   c. To provide expectations about when the product or service can be delivered

3. **Deliver.** Once the ideas are built, a customized product or service can be delivered. The shorter time this step takes, the sooner the users can get started and the sooner the team can learn from the users.

4. **Use.** In this step, customers will use the real product; this is not a demo. During use, the team keeps a close eye on which and how much feedback the customer provides. Feedback can of course be both positive and negative. In addition, the customer can give hard and soft feedback. Hard feedback consists of data such as visitor numbers, conversion percentages, usage figures, and user percentage per region. Soft feedback is, for example, reactions submitted via e-mail, messages on social media, evaluations, customer visits, and interviews.

   This step ends when enough feedback has been received to process or when an agreed amount of time has elapsed. Usually a couple of days to a few weeks are allotted. But if after five minutes of use by the customer it appears that the product is not working, the next step can be taken immediately.

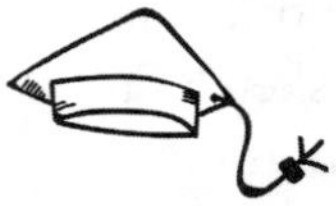

5. **Learn.** In this step, the focus is on learning. The team studies soft and hard feedback and thereby learns which ideas worked well in practice and which did not. As a result, the team grows, and it is always better to build products and services with which the customer is satisfied. In addition, the team can adjust or delete existing ideas and sketch new ideas based on the feedback.

   The learning loop has now been completed once, and the next cycle starts again at Step 1.

If we only knew about the existence of this learning loop in 2005 when creating the new product Revent. Then we would have received feedback from users much earlier and we could have made better decisions to improve the final product.

So how does the agile leader know whether his teams perform the qualitatively right work? It can be concluded that the learning loop is crucial to answer this question. Without a learning loop, it is impossible for an agile leader to know whether his teams are doing well. As the teams go through the learning loop, the agile leader gets real insight through feedback from end customers. If many users are often satisfied, it can be concluded that the teams are doing the right thing.

The Agile Leader as an Experimentor

Successful agile leaders support their teams and mentor them in running experiments. They create a safe environment where the teams can learn from mistakes, experiments, and tryouts. The outcomes of the experiments are also proudly shared with other departments and upper management—even when the outcome is negative and has (some) bad consequences. These leaders have teams that apply this learning loop in their daily work. The role of the agile leader is that of experimentor; he acts as the mentor of the experiments so that the team can learn quickly and safely.

- Coach the team to go through each step of the learning loop. Do not skip steps or take steps too quickly because of time pressure.
- Ensure that the team is not working harder just to achieve their short-term results, but rather obtains feedback from users.
- Inspire the team to have an open mind for this feedback. Don't stick to assumptions, suspicions, and opinions. Rather, ask questions and be open to refreshing ideas from customers.
- Explain why structurally reporting on user satisfaction and usage is so important.
- When the users are highly satisfied, give the team all the appreciation and gratitude. They are very mature and need a lot of freedom to be motivated (see Part 2, "Facilitate Ownership").
- If user satisfaction is low, first pose a lot of open questions to the team, helping, guiding, and—if necessary—making adjustments to increase user satisfaction.
- Brainstorm with the teams on the impediments for next steps to a smooth and faster learning loop. Remove these obstacles or give the team a mandate to remove them by themselves. Often, obstacles reside in part with other employees or departments. That is why it is important to look for cooperation and to make decisions together with fellow managers.

3.2 HOW QUICKLY DO MY TEAMS LEARN FROM USERS?

In a complex, unpredictable, and dynamic market, it's crucial that teams know quickly whether they are doing the right work.

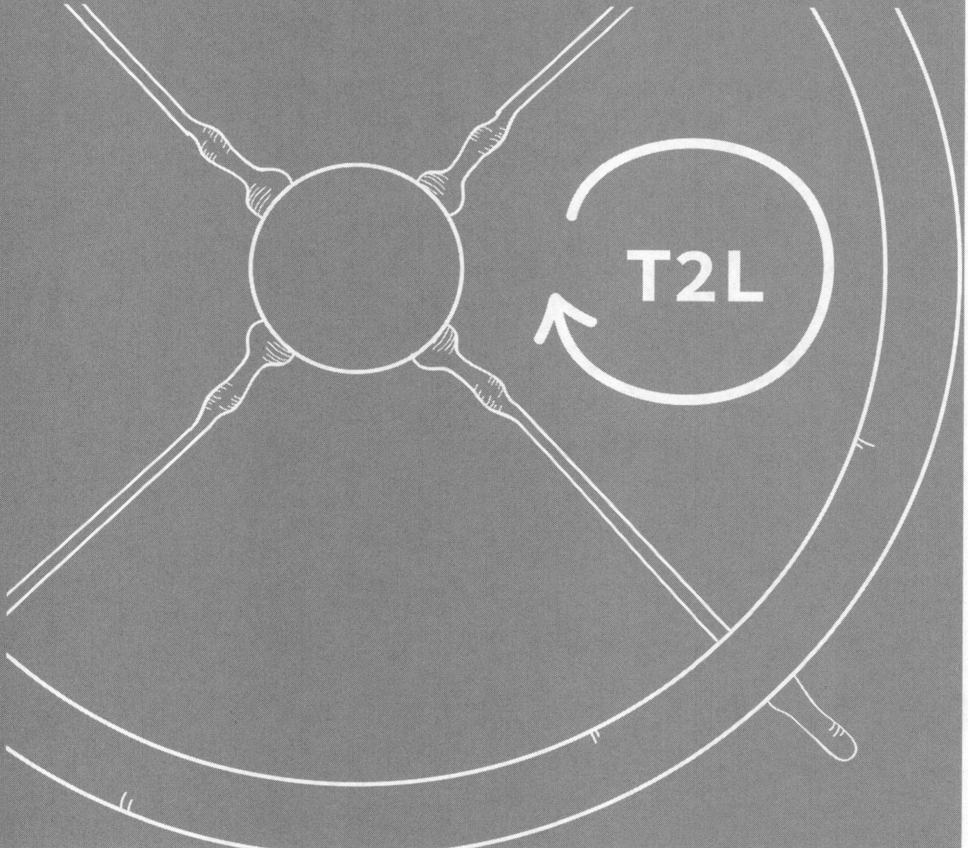

Introduction Questions

1. Lately, what do users give as feedback?
2. How much time is spent per week on learning from actual usage?

The learning loop provides insight into whether the teams are doing the right thing. But does this insight come quickly enough? Is feedback requested quickly enough? It is not possible that the teams will only know in a year's time whether they are doing the right thing today. This can be compared to driving for half an hour blindfolded or, as a cook, not wanting to know whether guests like the food. In a complex, unpredictable, and dynamic market, it is crucial that teams know quickly whether they are doing the right work. They have to know whether what they make is still in line with the rapidly changing needs. It is therefore important that the learning loop is completed quickly—in other words, to have a high learning speed. The sooner and more quickly it becomes clear whether teams are doing the right thing, the better teams can respond to unexpected situations. But can this speed be measured? And if so, how?

Tool 5: T2L

There is a good way to determine how quickly the feedback from users is processed or how high the learning speed of a team is. For this we measure how long it takes to go through Steps 2 through 5 of the learning loop (i.e., from "Build" through "Learn"). This time is called the time to learn (T2L).

T2L Time to learn (T2L) is the total time needed from sketching an idea or improvement, building it, bringing it to the users, and learning from their usage.

The T2L includes refining and designing, developing, testing, and integrating it, deploying it to market, letting users actually use it, gathering statistics and feedback on that usage, studying these results, and actually learning from it.

This metric is based on the lead-time metric often used in manufacturing and the time-to-market metric. These metrics measure the internal process until just before the customer receives it. They don't incorporate the feedback and data from actual users. In complex environments, this feedback is crucial to know whether the market has changed and how to continuously improve the actual customer impact. It's the role of the agile leader to improve the environment of his teams so that they can learn faster.

The shorter the T2L, the greater the learning speed. This is comparable to traveling from Amsterdam to Paris. The shorter the travel time, the higher the speed must have been. So by shortening the T2L, the learning speed is increased. By improving the T2L, the teams learn faster from actual usage.

Figure 3.2 show some examples of calculating the T2L.

	Build	Deliver	Use	Learn	T2L
1	5 months	1 month	3 months	1 month	10 months
2	2 months	0,5 month	2 months	0,5 month	5 months
3	4 weeks	0 days	1 week	1 week	6 weeks

Figure 3.2 Calculating T2L

In the first example, the T2L is ten months. To make this concrete, if a management team makes the strategic choice to put a new product on the market in early February, they will know in mid-November whether they have made the right decision. Only then will enough feedback from real users be processed. Before that time, they made decisions based on opinions and assumptions. If they then make choices for a few improvements in mid-November, it will take another ten months before they have learned again. That is why it is important that the management team focus on shortening the T2L. By implementing improvements in a few places, the T2L can be lowered relatively quickly. Some examples are as follows:

- By choosing a smaller customer group instead of solving everything for everyone, the construction step becomes significantly shorter (see Section 3.4 for more examples).
- Because the solution is less extensive, feedback from users can often be collected more quickly.
- By placing focus across departments and, in particular, reducing idle and waiting times, the turnaround time is considerably reduced.

In the preceding example, the T2L can be shortened relatively easily to five months.

Higher Agility through Shorter T2L

Companies that have a long T2L will receive feedback from users about their strategic choices months or even years later. Companies with a short T2L can have that much earlier. The higher the learning speed, the faster companies can respond to developments. So the shorter the T2L, the higher the strategic agility of the organization. The agility of an organization is determined by the time it takes to change direction plus the time required to know whether this is a good change. Without the latter, the organization will change direction randomly and blindly. Agile companies are able to change direction quickly and then quickly get feedback on the new course.

T2L in Practice

How can the T2L be taken into practice? First of all, by including this standard in the various weekly and monthly reports of, for example, projects, improvement initiatives, team overviews, and products. This creates much more focus on improving the learning speed.

For this, it is useful to steer on a low T2L when making the plans. By choosing a phased rollout and not doing everything at once, the T2L is already considerably lower. In addition, it is a good indication of the risk for projects: a low T2L means a lower risk. There is more feedback from real users, which makes it clear more quickly if a project is feasible and valuable.

What is a good relationship between the duration of a project, initiative or improvement, and the corresponding T2L? For a project with an expected lead time of twelve months, a T2L of three months is pleasant. The shorter the better. For a project with a duration of four months, a T2L of one month is a good start. A T2L of one-fourth the lead time is often a good rule of thumb. In practice, medium-sized companies initially often have a T2L from nine months to more than a year. Before they start measuring and improving the T2L, these are recognizable numbers. Companies that have already made structural improvements for some time have a T2L of two to four months. Highly mature agile teams that issue releases to users several times a week have a T2L of less than one month.

It can be concluded that with the T2L, the learning speed of teams can be measured. This figure indicates how quickly agile teams learn. Lowering the T2L increases the learning speed. A lower T2L is therefore an improvement. The T2L is a handy tool that allows the agile leader to have control over the organization. It is also a good indicator to help teams know quickly whether they are doing the right thing. By including the T2L in matters such as reports, improvement initiatives, and projects, it is also applied and used in practice. It is the agile leader's job to make the T2L transparent and to ensure that it is improved.

Steering on the T2L has four additional advantages that emphasizes the importance of a good T2L.

Four Additional Benefits of a Better T2L

There are four additional benefits of a better T2L.

Advantage 1: Lower Cost-of-Delay

If an analyst or programmer continues his morning work after lunch, he only needs a few minutes to get back to the topic. On the other hand, if he picks up work from a few weeks ago, it takes much more time to dive into the topic and recall all of the details. So, the more time that passes before he resumes work, the longer it takes for him to do so. For thought work, creative tasks, and unique activities, this is a latent cost that managers aren't aware of; it's the *cost-of-delay*. The longer things are paused or idle, the more expensive it becomes to pick them up again. The problem with this cost-of-delay is that it can hardly be measured. Indirectly, measurement can be achieved by measuring the difference between lead time and time spent. If something takes forty hours to make but it has taken two months, there is probably a significant cost-of-delay.

Lowering the T2L therefore automatically lowers the cost-of-delay. Work is quickly delivered to customers and quickly learned from, and therefore improvements can be made quickly. The employees involved need to delve much less often into topics in which they were engaged a while ago. They therefore have a much lower cost-of-delay.

Advantage 2: Lower Cost-of-Change

"We have already invested so much, we better continue." "Couldn't you say that earlier? Then I would not have had to redo this all over again!" "Now that I know this, a simpler solution would have also worked." These are familiar phrases. As soon as months have been invested in a new product or expansion, stopping is more difficult than when much less effort has been invested. After all, if something has to be built in a different way, both the current way has to be taken out and the new way brought in. We call this double cost the *cost-of-change* (change costs). If a decision is made to change a product completely after just three months, very different amounts will be involved than if this is not decided until after ten months. That is why a better T2L also results in a lower cost-of-change.

Advantage 3: Higher Team Motivation

A team worked intensively together last week to make delivery possible. At the start of this week, they received enthusiastic feedback from users. This was very exciting. Imagine another team that got this feedback months later. This results in demotivation or passiveness. An improved T2L benefits motivation and cooperation in the team. They already have ideas for the next delivery. In addition, customers now see the results of their feedback in the new increment more quickly. Their ideas have been incorporated in the functionalities and services. As a result, the cooperation with customers has improved considerably, and the team receives much more valuable feedback. A lower T2L contributes to increased team motivation.

Advantage 4: Improved Liquidity

A T2L that is too long can be compared to too large a stock in a factory: it results in lower liquidity. The items have already been bought but have not yet been sold. As a result, there is a lot of money in stock at the warehouse, which could have been in the bank. The same applies to the work of teams that have not yet been sold. Employees have already spent a lot of time creating or adapting new products and services, but these are still in the warehouse, as it were. The labor has not yet been sold. The T2L gives a good indication of this stock of unsold labor. By multiplying the T2L with the internal cost price, the stock becomes transparent. The T2L indicates the moment when we received feedback from customers and learned from the time spent. So by lowering the T2L, liquidity can be increased because the time when products and services generate money is brought forward.

In the next section, I explain how teams can make their work more transparent every day and thus learn even more quickly.

3.3 HOW CAN THE LEARNING LOOP BE PUT INTO PRACTICE?

I just recycle my good intentions from last year.

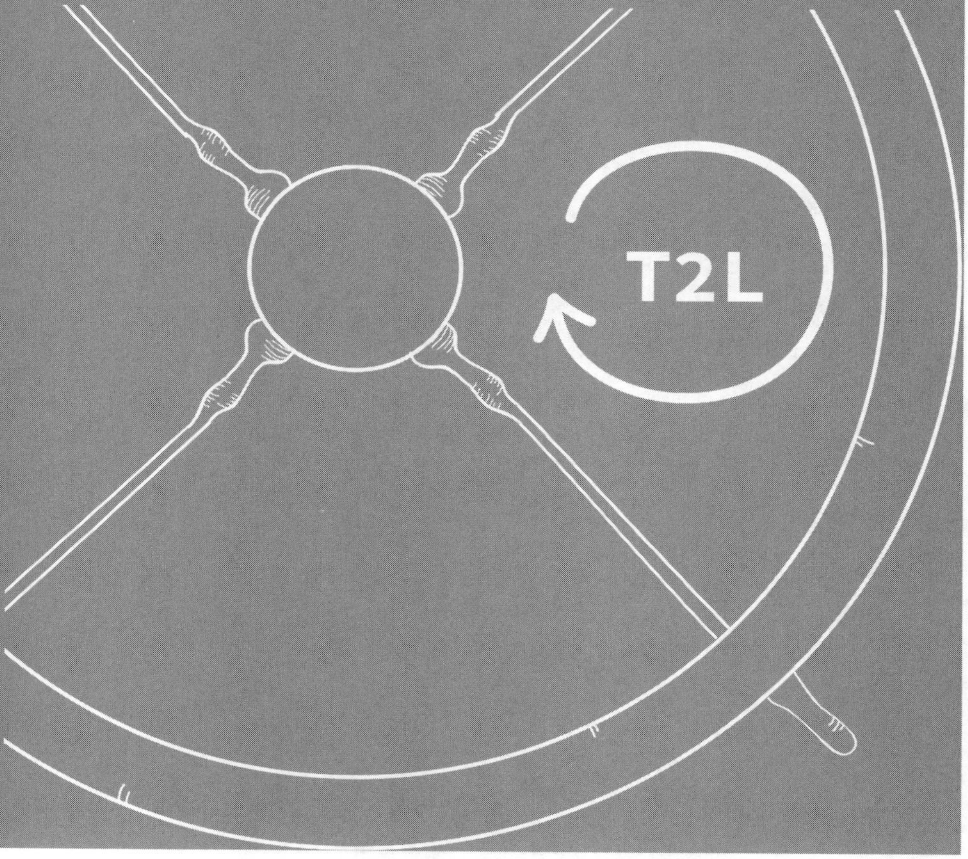

Introduction Questions

T2L
LEARN
Faster

1. Where is the feedback from users collected?
2. Is the progress of the learning loop visually monitored?

In recent years, I have been looking for a practical tool for teams to work with the learning loop every day. The tool I was seeking had to help teams to be focused on learning in their daily work, getting feedback from users, and quickly adjusting to the latest insights. The learning loop and the shortening of the T2L are important, but little use was made in real life. Ultimately, this led to the creation of the Validated Learning Board (VLB). This board records an overview of the activities per step of the learning loop (Figure 3.3). As soon as one of the activities enters the learning loop in a next step, the board is updated by moving the corresponding card. The board can be a physical overview on the wall or a digital board in a tool. A physical board often increases the interaction and involvement of the entire team.

If stakeholders and customers are updated about products and services, the board is also used to make an overall overview of the learning loop. This allows stakeholders and customers to quickly understand the ideas the team is working on, what is done with their feedback, and what lessons have been learned.

By using the board both daily to plan activities and during consultations with stakeholders and customers, the VLB becomes a practical tool for agile teams to work with the learning loop on a daily basis and improve their T2L. The VLB is a Kanban board but not for the internal process only; its purpose is to visualize the work over the complete learning loop.

Tool 6: VLB

To make the learning loop concrete, a simple and effective overview is required. Having this overview is crucial because, in real life, it becomes complicated pretty quickly—at the same time that users are trying out new functionalities, other things are being built and new ideas are being sketched. So the challenge here is that a product or service is simultaneously in different steps of the learning loop. The VLB clearly shows what is in which step of the learning loop.

The VLB consists of six columns, with each column representing a step in the learning loop—sketching, building, delivering, using, and learning (see Figure 3.3). Finally, there is a final column labeled "Done" or "Learned." In each column, these activities are current for the teams that are in that specific phase of the learning cycle. Ideally, there is a VLB per product or service. If many teams work together on a product or service, it is practical to also make a VLB for each team.

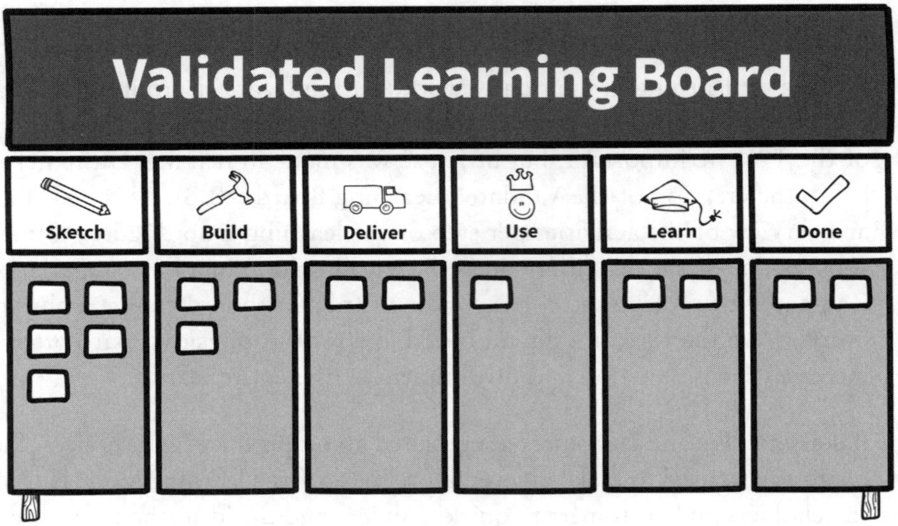

Figure 3.3 Validated Learning Board

As soon as an idea or functionality goes to a next step of the learning loop, it is immediately updated on the board. As a result, the board is always up-to-date. Colleagues or customers get a quick picture of the current status of the learning loop.

THE CARD ON THE BOARD

A card on the board often looks like what is shown in Figure 3.4.

Short description User story: As <**user**> I want <functionality> so that <benefit>			*Theme*
Date started	*Date delivered*	*Date learned*	*# Tool*

Figure 3.4 A card on the VBL

Each card contains the following elements:

- **Short description.** A few words indicate what matters, such as "Reporting for Families" or "Forgot password" or "Dashboard for first users."
- **User story.** One or two sentences with a little more explanation for readability. It can be assumed that stakeholders know what it is about. The power lies in being quickly readable, not in the details. These are included in the tool for the complete work stock (e.g., Excel, TFS, Jira, or Trello).
- **Theme.** Often, cards refer to a specific theme, such as "Good first impression" or "Simple reporting." It's best if the theme is visualized with an icon that increases recognizability. Or colored cards can also be used.
- **Date started, Date delivered, Date learned.** It is practical to keep three dates. For example, the T2L of this card can be calculated afterward.
- **# Tool.** The ID in the tool, with which you can quickly find more details.

How Detailed Should the VLB Be?

The work listed on the VLB is not very detailed but is on the level of larger pieces of work—so, not per column of the report or per button of the screen, but more per part of a theme. This is to prevent huge quantities of cards and keep the overview reliable. Let the level of detail depend on the current T2L. If the T2L lasts for six months, there are tickets for a larger theme on the board. If the T2L is only a few months, there may be more cards with details on the board.

Common Place, Close to the Team

The best place for a VLB is on a common wall, close to the team—for example, in a hallway near the team, or in the regular consultation room of the team with all kinds of overviews, such as the roadmap, statistics, KVI, improvement initiatives, etc. Invite stakeholders and customers to visit the board.

STAKEHOLDERS AND CUSTOMERS MEETING

With the VLB, we now have a tool to make the learning loop practical and concrete. But with the VLB, the full strength of the learning loop is not yet put into practice. For this, it is important that time is regularly spent on learning together with stakeholders and customers. A structural meeting on the content of the VLB helps with this. If Scrum is used, add the following parts to the sprint review event. In other cases, it is good to have an interactive event on a regular basis, the *T2L event,* which lasts a maximum of two hours.

GOAL T2L EVENT

The goal of the T2L event is to improve the list of ideas so that the next version of a product or service is even better. In addition, this event aims to shorten the T2L by removing obstacles and increasing cooperation. During the T2L event, the latest insights, learning points, and ideas are incorporated in the list. In addition, improvements are being looked at to increase the learning speed. All agile teams come up with ideas to implement improvements in the process, reducing the turnaround time.

HOW OFTEN TO HAVE A T2L EVENT?

A practical rule of thumb is to hold a T2L event every two weeks. It is useful to look at the frequency of delivery. For example, if something is delivered to users once every two months, it makes less sense to look at the learning loop every two weeks. If, on the other hand, delivery occurs every day, this event can be held more often and will probably take less time.

WHEN AND WITH WHOM?

For example, the T2L event takes place on Thursday in the even weeks, between 2 and 4 p.m. Present are the product manager, the team coach, and the team(s) that work(s) together on the same product or service. Preferably, users are also invited. The agile leader is optional; this is an event of the agile team. The agile leader can indicate the importance of this event with his presence and help to implement actions quickly. However, mature teams should be able to hold this event autonomously without any guidance of the leader (see the Ownership Model in Part 2).

In Preparation

The team has prepared well for this learning session. They have taken the time to study the feedback and have already drawn preliminary conclusions. A brief overview of this has already been sent to the other participants for preparation.

- The ultimate goal is repeated: what are the measurable ambitions and KVI for this product or service? (See Part 1, "Co-Create Goals.")
- The most important figures and trendlines are briefly explained.
- The current average T2L is announced, along with some possible improvements to shorten it.
- An agenda includes the hard numbers and the soft feedback on actual usage indicated for each subject in more detail. Consider figures on conversion, time, number of customers, percentage of the target group, etc., and comments from customers or explanations of interviews.

Power of the Validated Learning Board

It can be concluded that the VLB is a powerful tool to continuously work within the learning loop, on a daily basis, and really apply it. The strength lies in the fact that the teams work with it daily, visualize their work, and also use the tool to continuously learn and improve together with stakeholders and customers.

The agile leader has the following tasks:

- Indicate the importance of the board and the event.
- Engage with the team on a regular basis and ask questions about the progress of the learning loop.
- Motivate the team to repeat the lessons learned and pass them on to other teams.
- Ensure that impediments of the learning speed are removed.
- Facilitate the right stakeholders and customers, keeping time free to be present at the T2L event.
- Support product managers in stakeholder management.

After all of this explanation about the learning loop, measuring the learning speed, and the VLB, the question remains: how can large ideas be implemented in small steps? Are not enormous risks taken due to speed? Are changes made safely? The following two sections provide answers to these challenges.

3.4 HOW CAN TEAMS IMPLEMENT BIG IDEAS IN SMALL STEPS?

The man who moves mountains begins by carrying away small stones.

– Confucius

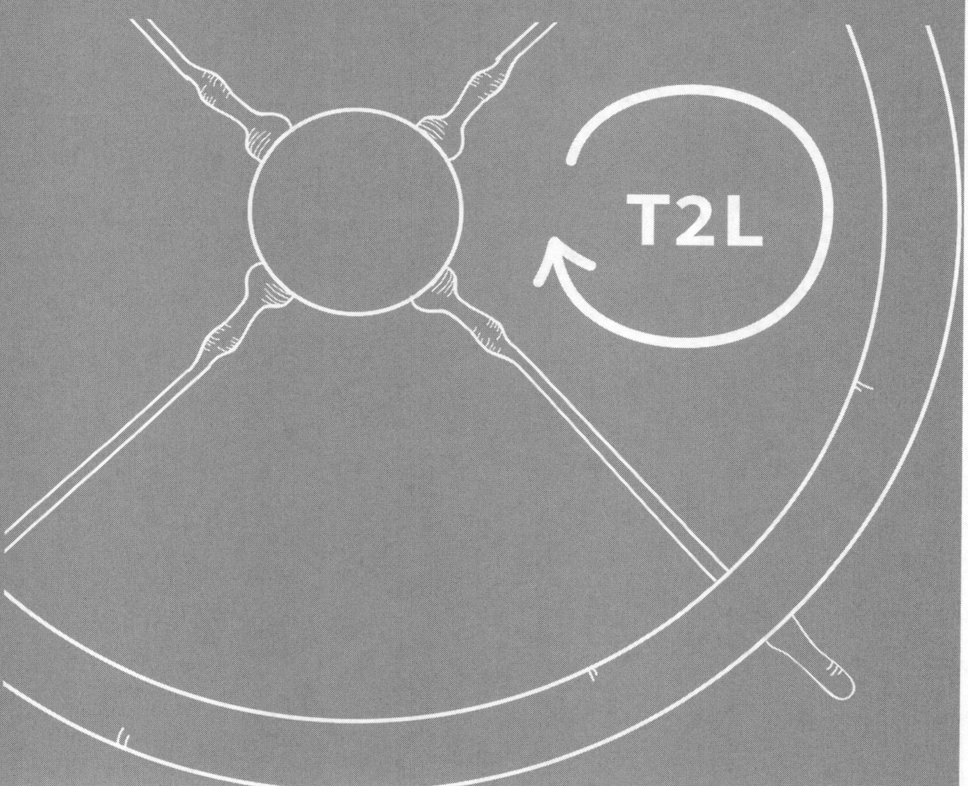

Introduction Questions

1. How long does it take before a big new idea is validated with users?
2. When are big important ideas stopped or killed because of user feedback?

Introduction Story

A roadside assistance organization had to replace the software for coordinating aid in order to remain a market leader. A team of analysts and experts set to work on the requirements, functional design, and starting architecture. After more than six months of meetings, writing, reviewing, and planning, they presented their results to senior management, who agreed with the rebuilding of the internal product. According to the plans, it would take several years to build the new system and months of intensive testing. A few critical project leaders found that to be too much risk for a crucial part of the operation. Fortunately, one of them knew the then still relatively unknown mindset of agile project management. In terms of planning, they decided to completely change the approach: not just go live when everything was built, but as soon as a specific target group and situation could be supported. The new plan was to go live in parallel. A large part of the daily support staff would use the current system and a handful of others would have access to both systems. After a fierce discussion with the steering group, the new method was given a serious chance. One comment was decisive: "If we continue to do what we always did, we get what we got. We have a low chance of success for such large projects. Now we know in three months whether it works and otherwise only in three years...."

The biggest challenge was to find a way to put out something live within two months and learn from actual usage. After an intensive brainstorming session in which several scenarios were discussed, an idea was rolled out to shorten the T2L from three years to three months. As soon as customers called for a specific breakdown or problem, the support staff could use the new system for the new cases and the current one for all other cases. Ultimately, it was decided to let the new system be the first to deal with a flat tire in Germany with a Ford. The telephone system could be configured so that phone calls on behalf of Ford drivers from Germany were forwarded to the support staff who used both systems. As a result, the new system did not have to be installed for all hundreds of support staff, but only for four people. These were also the only ones that needed to be trained and incorporated into the new functionality. As soon as the telephone rang, the support employee could know within a few seconds whether the specific case was supported by the new system. This was a perfect solution so they could go live in two months! Gradually more situations would be supported after the initial release.

The first version naturally contained input screens, but no new functionality needed to be created for planning and coordinating the emergency services. A link with the German colleagues was sufficient, and then the German road guards could continue to deal with it. After a few weeks of construction, the first version was ready. This was rolled out for the four support staff, and the first calls could be handled—a great moment for the project.

After a few releases and improvements of the overall learning loop, they had a T2L of an average of one-and-a-half months: two weeks of sketching, two weeks of building, and two weeks of collecting and learning from user data. The original plan would have had a T2L of more than three years!

In the end, no more than 70% of the functionalities that analysts, experts, and architects had built up were being built. And more than 25% of the functionalities were ultimately much simpler and completely different than originally planned.

SPLIT INTO TARGET GROUP AND SITUATIONS, NOT INTO PARTS AND FUNCTIONALITY

People often ask how they can properly divide an idea, large project, new product, or service. They want to deliver earlier to customers and ask for feedback, but they do not know how to make parts effectively smaller. Making these cuts intelligently ensures that products or services can actually be used more effectively in practice. A common mistake is to immediately want to support all possible target groups and almost all functionalities. In the end, only real feedback can be retrieved when it works. Cutting up a project well is sometimes difficult in practice. It takes time to find a solution together for that specific situation. Tip: choose the user target group and the situation in which this target group can already use the product. The following are some practical examples.

ASSISTANCE

In the example of the roadside assistance described earlier, a real choice was made in the target group and situation. In the first instance, not all assistance situations could be supported in Germany. As soon as someone called in Germany for an empty battery or lost key, for example, the current system had to be used. The same was true when someone from the Netherlands or France called.

TRAVEL INDUSTRY

An example for the travel industry is to make a new product or service first available to people who want to go to southern Spain and southern Portugal.

Then by making further splits for a specific target group—for example, people older than 60, or the time during which travel occurs, namely, before and after tourist season. The first target group and situation is then "travelers over 60 years old who want to enjoy the sun in the early or late seasons in southern Spain or southern Portugal." This also immediately provides the advantage that not all kinds of exception functionalities need to be built. For example, there is no need to take into account transit, stopovers, tours, combination discounts, and visa applications. Improper cutting would first make the new service available when searching for travel but not when booking travel. After all, all kinds of exception functionalities must be built immediately. This means that the entire process would not be able to be completed quickly because no feedback from end users would be available. Effective cutting in target groups and situations makes this possible.

Legislative Change of Benefits

To comply with a new law, all benefits must be recalculated from January 1. The implementation, testing, and rollout of all changes takes more than nine months so it could not possibly be completed before January 1. In retrospect it sounds simple, but at the time it took hours and several sessions of experts, law analysts, programmers, functional managers, and project leaders to get the idea. An overview was made per category of benefits and the complexity of the new calculation. The benefit to single mothers with children living at home turned out to be the easiest and a large amount of benefits. Halfway through the list was the benefit to self-employed people, and the most difficult cases were combinations of disabled, unemployed, and groups of related and unrelated persons living together.

The team first decided to implement the benefit for single mothers. After about a month, the functionality could be delivered to the users. These users could therefore directly indicate when calculating the benefit whether it should be according to the future or the current calculation. However, the package did not yet comply with the law. The requirement was that all payments had to be properly handled. By incorporating that the benefit handler could set the amount himself, they strictly complied with the law. This initially met with resistance from a few stakeholders, which was partially bridged by the promise to continue to implement new calculations. The stakeholders realized that it was therefore much easier to work together to determine the order of installation of calculations. Reducing the workload of the daily operation was used as the most important argument.

Although on January 1 part of the calculations was not automated, it worked out well in practice. The last few benefit categories were so difficult that the probability that the right payment was calculated was relatively low. As a result, these benefits always had to be recalculated by a benefit expert. This allowed the team to gain experience with how they could support benefit experts. Eventually they built a tool for easy checking of the calculations, which increased the number of correct benefits.

Legislation on Mortgages

A medium-sized mortgage service provider had to adjust its systems because of legislative changes around mortgages. A first analysis indicated that they would have to deal with hundreds of difficult combinations. After a brainstorming session, they decided to implement the amendment of the law in parts. First of all, they would include the changes for all mortgages below 70% of the value of the house with one loan component and one owner. At that point, the change was relatively simple and the situations could easily be removed from the system. The adapted letters and process steps were delivered to customers fairly quickly. This allowed the teams to both gain experience with the new law and to receive feedback from real customers about their experience. This made it easier for them to make an outline of the other situations and thus manage the expectations of stakeholders and higher management. So they expanded the number of situations step by step. Although they were unable to support all situations before the new law came into effect, that resulted in minimal problems for financial regulators.

Pitfalls When Shortening the T2L

Shortening the T2L has some pitfalls. If this happens indiscriminately, the number of risks can rise.

Pitfall 1: A Select Customer Group

At an energy company, all kinds of customers were asked to participate in a customer panel that was the first to use new products and services. It was explained that some products and services might soon be stopped again, depending mainly on the customers' feedback. Much has been communicated about the feedback from this customer panel, both among employees and toward customers. It was a real step forward for the company to involve customers at an early stage in their development. Unfortunately, the customer panel did not appear to be a random representation of the total customer population. Rather than consisting of hard-working double-income households and young families, the panel consisted mainly of pensioners, young people without work, and very environmentally conscious rich people in their 40s. This group was happy to make time available for the public benefit and therefore was more aware of their energy spending every day. Unfortunately, the average customer of the energy company was not. As a result, the company made wrong choices about their products and services. In the end, the customer panel was maintained, but the feedback was less decisive in the choices. Marketing intelligence experts were also used to get more random customer feedback.

When shortening the T2L, it is therefore important to use as random a user group as possible. Tip: let an expert in statistics have a look at the user group.

Pitfall 2: Performance Test on Current Numbers

Five different software development teams started a complete rebuild of an existing product. They focused on a specific target group and on a specific situation, which enabled them to actually go live within a few months. They knew at the start that in the summer their product would be used minimally, but in the winter it would be used by thousands of simultaneous users. They had taken this into account in the architecture. However, during the construction—on the basis of new insights—small changes were implemented in the architecture. Nobody expected that this would have major consequences for the performance. When scaling up to more users, unexpectedly, such high performance problems arose that part of the product had to be redesigned and rebuilt. This was obviously a big disappointment, and several stakeholders questioned the strength of the agile process. The teams then learned the hard way to execute performance tests after each change. In the months and years after, when the team expanded the product, they were warned in time about changes that had a negative impact on performance.

When shortening the T2L, it is therefore important that (automatic) tests are done on the future level of demand. Tip: let an expert in performance tests review or consult the teams.

PITFALL 3: REQUEST FEEDBACK WHEN IT IS FINISHED

An important rule of thumb for agile work is "Do not wait for feedback until something is finished, but ask for feedback because it's time for feedback." We are inclined to ask for feedback only when we are done. This rule challenged me during a 10-minute conversation at my daughter's elementary school. The teacher gave all kinds of compliments to our daughter—how smart she is and that she participates well in the class. At the end of the conversation, the teacher unexpectedly said that our daughter was sometimes a bit insecure. A few days before, the children were asked to make a mushroom. The teacher had given a clear explanation for this, and everyone went to work. Our daughter, after a few minutes, came to the teacher with a half-finished drawing of a mushroom in her hands. That gave the teacher the impression that she was insecure.

Already, as early as elementary school, we learn to ask for feedback when something is finished. It is not possible to ask the teacher halfway through the language or math test whether she would like to check a part so that we can make the second part better. Experts are also used to this more traditional way of working. Excellent experts only need half the story to understand the problem and find the solution. Feedback questions about ongoing research, an analysis, or calling a customer is quickly seen as a proof of uncertainty. Because the world is becoming increasingly complex and machines and computers take care of the simple things (see Part 1), interaction between people is increasingly taking place around a complex problem.

While reducing the T2L, it is very important that we ask for a lot of feedback midway through and not wait until the project is finished.

Pitfall 4: Staff Discount

Many companies give their employees discounts on products and services—discount on the mortgage, a free membership, or a 20% discount for friends and family. Although this has all kinds of positive effects, it also causes a colored opinion of a customer group that is involved everywhere. For example, would their own employees also use the products or services if they did not receive a discount? The personnel discount ensures that employees who are intensively involved in the products and services themselves can more objectively ask themselves whether they would also buy them.

In other words, an easily accessible customer group is no longer objective, and employees must go outside to get feedback. The latter is obviously good anyway, but it would be easier if employees also formed a customer group.

3.5 MINIMIZE THE BLAST RADIUS

Without a safe environment in which to experiment, we will only optimize what we already do. And this results in standing still in an accelerating market.

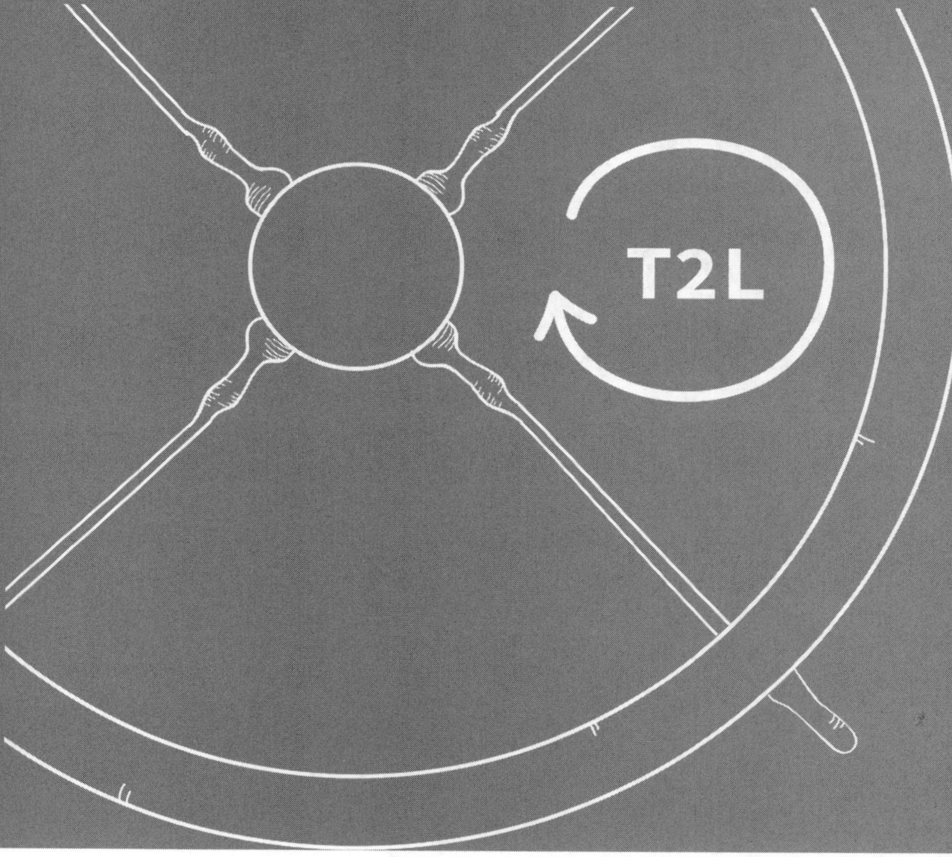

Introduction Questions

1. How much time is spent on experimenting?
2. How much freedom and inspiration does your team feel to experiment?

At Spotify, they have a practical way to reduce the impact of errors: preventing a certain error from having an impact on all users. They reduce the *blast radius*.[1] All changes that are put in production are gradually rolled out across all customers. For example, they might be rolled out first in the United Kingdom, next only in the United States. In addition, they use *feature toggles*, with which changes can be turned on and off without a rollback. They turn on the feature for a certain number of users in a specific country. Through user statistics, they can quickly see if the feature works and if they like it. If this is not the case, they will switch the feature off again. Should a feature lead to errors, then only a small user group suffers from it.

The consequences of an error can thus be limited by not implementing the improvement for all customers at the same time, but only for a small target group. Or it can be limited by not directly adjusting everything, but only a few products or services. Various companies have been applying this for years. Some examples include the following:

- New versions of a banking app are first rolled out to employees before they become available to a wider audience. If something does not work well, the consequences are relatively small.
- A telephone company does not adapt all transmitter masts simultaneously for 4G but starts with one transmitter mast in, for example, the center of Houston. Customers can use 4G there first. The fact that not all data was included in the data bundle obviously did not bother customers. The consequences for the telephone company were small.

To reduce the consequences of an error, it is often necessary to change the design of products and services. Although it is often very pleasant to treat everything in the same way from a standardization, cost reduction, and efficiency perspective and to not to allow exceptions, this is not useful in view of improvements, risk reduction, and innovation.

It is therefore important to look at this challenge from different perspectives with various employees. Several brainstorming sessions can be held for this

1. https://hbr.org/2017/02/how-spotify-balances-employee-autonomy-and-accountability

purpose in order to reflect together on possible structural improvements in working methods, processes, automation, and collaboration.

If All Changes Are Successful, Insufficient Innovation Will Take Place

Successful agile leaders create an environment in which improvements can be explored and discovered. In this voyage of discovery, not every change is immediately a success. Without improvements you will stand still, but if other market players improve, you could even deteriorate! However, in a complex environment, it can't be predicted whether a change will be successful. Experimentation has to be done to address this issue. If racecar driver Max Verstappen and his team do not continuously make changes, he will be overtaken more and more often by the competition that does. Verstappen must continuously experiment with the car, the team appointments, the race process, and his own condition to at least keep up with its competitors.

If all changes are successful, insufficient innovation will take place. This is because when all the changed products and services are an immediate success, it's impossible to know whether innovation is taking place on the cutting edge. Only when a few products do not catch on do those companies discover the limits of innovation. If Max Verstappen does not occasionally take a corner too fast, he does not know whether he drives on the edge.

Successful agile leaders know that they have to innovate as much as possible and therefore have to constantly look for the limits. Nevertheless, improvements must not lead to insurmountable damage. Max Verstappen does not have to corner so fast that he ends up in hospital. Agile leaders must therefore create an environment in which they can safely experiment so that the cutting edge of innovation can be explored.

Summary of Part 3—Learn Faster

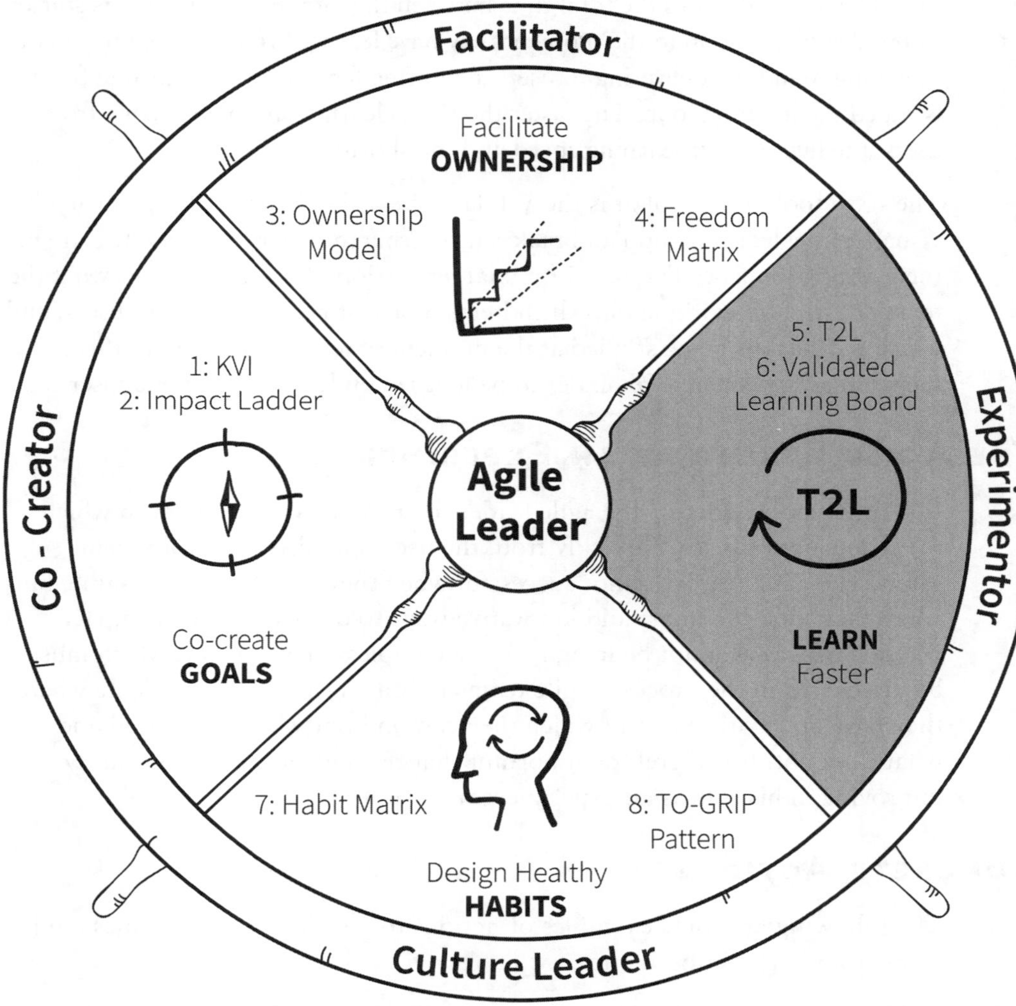

Agile teams need quick feedback from users, those who actually use the products and services in practice. This is not just feedback on ideas, presentations, or demos. Only through this practice test do teams know whether they are doing really well. See the figure shown here for the visualization of Part 3.

It is therefore important that the agile leader creates an environment in which the teams receive this feedback quickly and are given the opportunity to really learn from it. The T2L, the fifth tool of the toolkit for agile leaders, helps with this. This tool measures the total time between the moment the team has started to build something up to the moment they have learned from it. The process of sketching, building, delivering to users, collecting feedback, and learning from it is called the learning loop. The faster the teams learn from the feedback from users, the higher their learning speed and the shorter the T2L.

The sixth tool in the toolkit is the Validated Learning Board (VLB), which visualizes the learning loop and makes it transparent where the activities are in the learning loop. See Figure 3.5 for a larger version. The board shows what the team is currently working on, which items have just been delivered to users, and which feedback is being studied at the moment to learn from it. With this tool, the team gets a concrete reminder to be focused on learning from real users.

The Agile Leader as an Experimentor

It is the responsibility of the agile leader to create an environment in which the teams not only learn quickly from the users but also can experiment safely. The agile teams are not successful when they do more of the same, but when they look for smart and innovative ways to deliver customer impact. These new ways cannot be imagined in a complex environment, which must be discovered in the process. Agile teams become faster and more agile when they have an environment in which they can find out what works well and what does not. It is therefore important that the agile leader is constantly improving in his role as an experimentor.

Concrete Actions

The following are some examples of actions to put the tools, examples, and ideas from Part 3 into practice.

1. Make an overview of the teams with their current T2L. This makes it known what the learning speed of the different teams is. Work with the teams to update this overview so they take ownership of it.
2. Regularly ask teams what they need to experiment more safely. Create an environment in which safe experiments are rewarded and valued.
3. Ask for examples of failed experiments. Make sure there is no shame about this, but that people with a dose of humor can share what they have learned.
4. Plan the first series of T2L events.

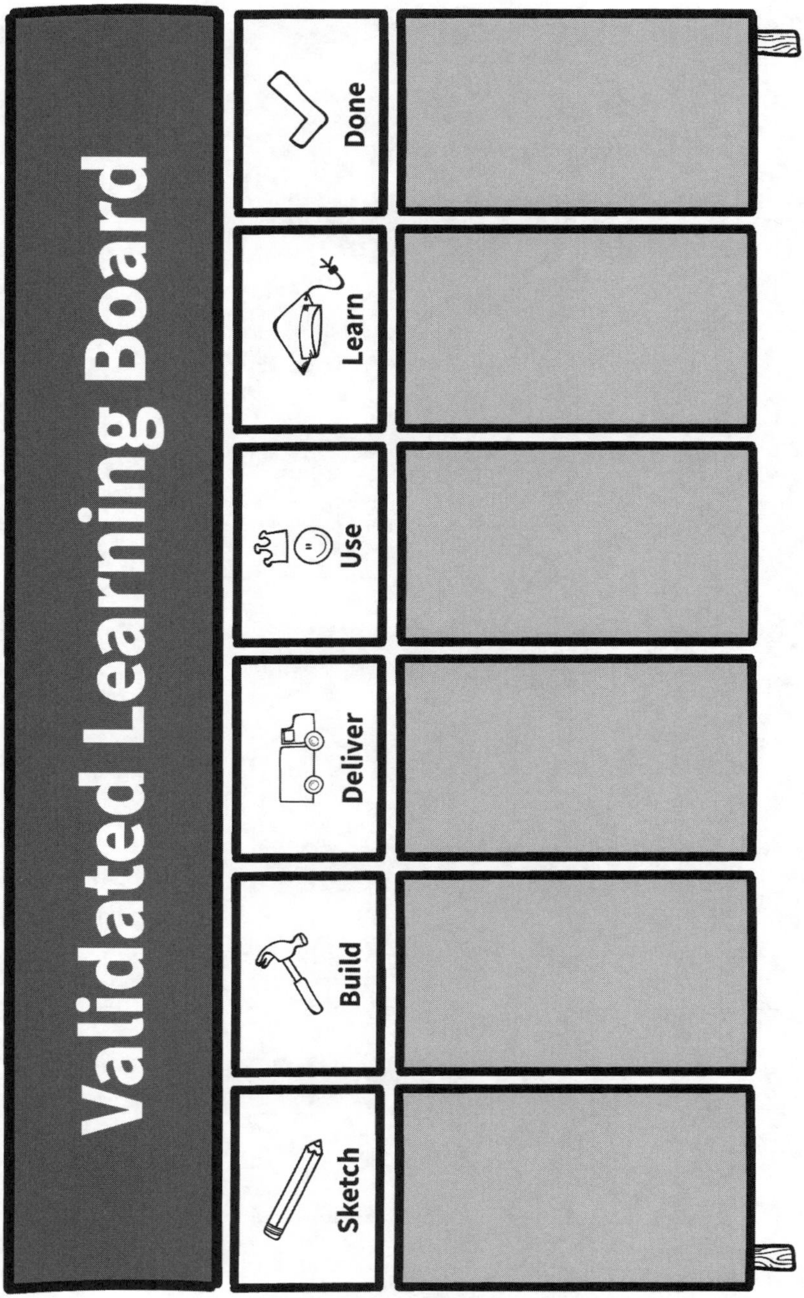

Figure 3.5 Validated Learning Board

Notes

PART 4
Design Healthy Habits

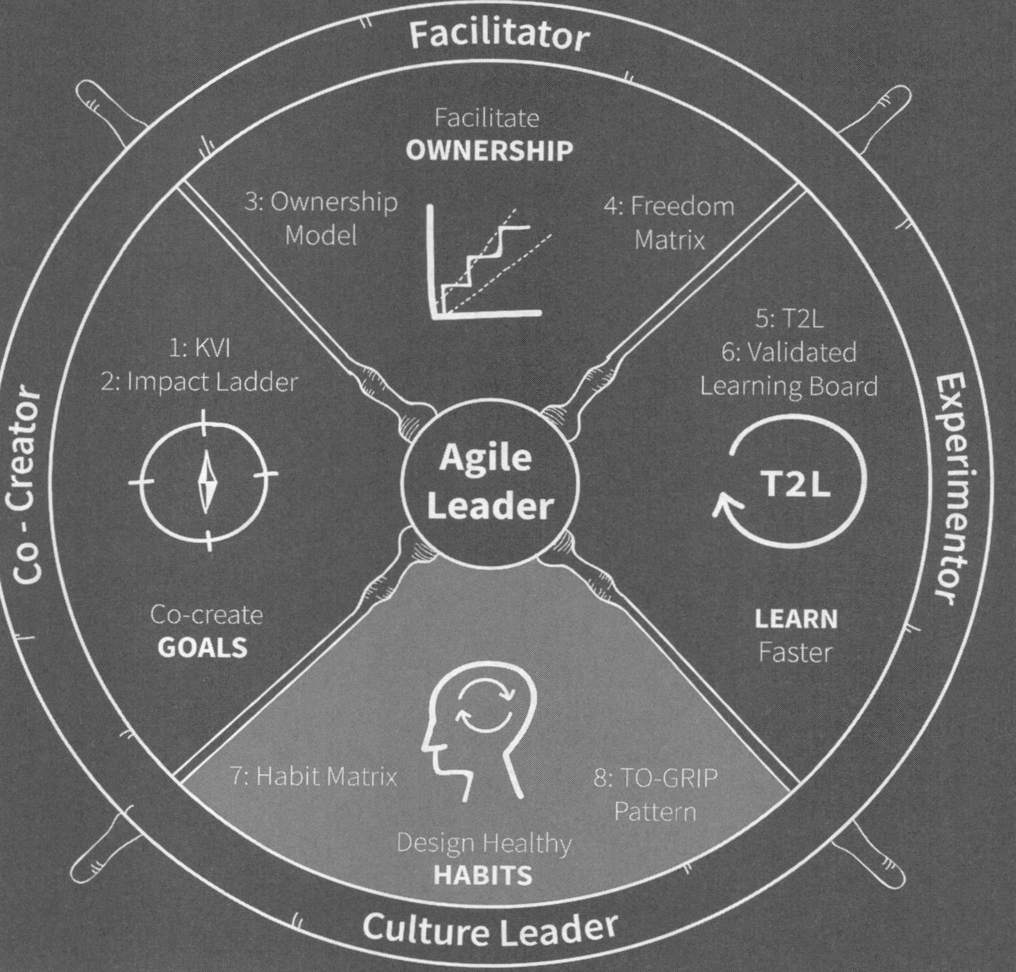

4.1 HOW DO YOU STIMULATE AN AGILE CULTURE?

The cultural health is solely in the hands of the leader. If he accepts that people go for self-interest and short-term results, lying, blaming others, or not sharing knowledge, this will become a habit and soon the culture.

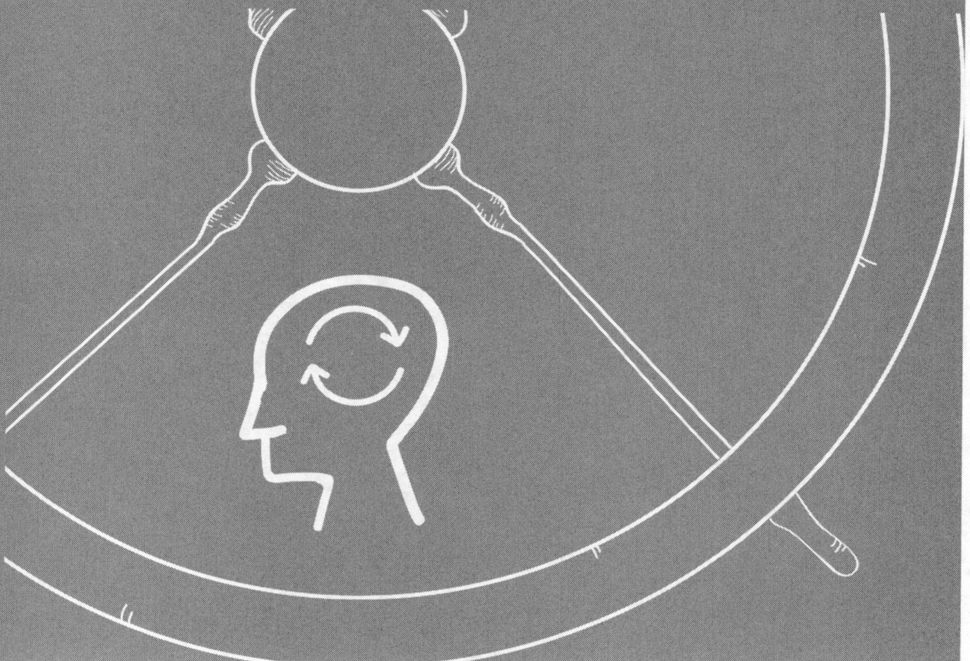

Introduction Questions

1. What are the most important characteristics of an agile culture for you?
2. Which role model do you want to be in the cultural change?

Introduction Story

It is after five. Rob, department director of the mid-office of a business bank, glares out the window. He has already put on his coat and tries to organize his thoughts. He knows intuitively that it is time for a next step, but he does not yet know exactly which step. In the background, he hears a few colleagues laughing; otherwise, it is quiet in the department. Most people are already home. Rob's department, with more than 400 employees, is responsible for handling financial files and dossiers. These files contain applications for new loans, extensions to existing loans, and a large diversity of mutations. Nine months ago, when he became a director, the department had to deal with a lot of backlogs, low quality, and unsatisfied customers. There was a demotivational culture in which people didn't help each other and had a habit of just putting in their hours without any extra effort. Fortunately, that has improved a bit already. Rob is satisfied with the cultural change so far, but he knows that there is still a lot of work to be done.

When Rob started working, employees were already in teams with different disciplines, which meant that as a team they were able to handle the entire dossier from beginning to end. Yet this structure was not sufficient because the daily practice was different. Each day every employee was busy with approving loans, returning files, or implementing mutations. Everyone tried as much as possible to get rid of their own work stock and to deliver the best possible quality.

In the meantime, Rob saw the backlogs and the complaints increase. If he did not turn the ship around, it would only get worse. His motto: "If you do what you did, you get what you got." Although everyone worked hard, the total output and quality were too low. Based on experience, Rob knew that this was not the caused by the culture, but by the structure and process. The lead time and handling time for a dossier differed enormously, not because people didn't want to work on a dossier but because different employees sent the dossier to each other to handle all kinds of details—which was according to the current process. This led to the situation that, after one month, customers heard that a few documents had not been properly filled in and that the whole process had to be redone. This led—of course—to low customer and employee satisfaction.

Rob felt intuitively that to change the culture he had to change the structure and the habits. He started with changing the habit around the work stock. He wanted to create the habit that all files that were received before 9:00 a.m. were handled the same day. Only then would the lead time probably improve customer and employee satisfaction. The first time he discussed his ideas, many people saw this as impossible. He was called "the next manager with wild ideas." But a few people saw the potential and started to work together with him on this new approach.

Together they ensured that the work stock was clear to everyone. This made it clear which teams had to process which files in a given day. Unlike in the past, the new overview only contained the files that were already in the working stock before 9:00 a.m. and not the files that had arrived in the course of the day. Because the teams were now tasked with finishing a file once they started to work on it, many teams immediately started to help each other. Very quickly, a different vibe and culture was sensed within the department.

The second thing Rob created, with help of his coalition, was a marketplace around 1:00 p.m. Teams who found out during the day that they could not get their job done could ask other teams for help during this marketplace. By mainly encouraging and rewarding the teams who had finished their work, the habit arose to ask for help. Teams who had finished their workload and did not need to help other teams were allowed to go home. This felt bad for the teams who had not asked for help and had to work. As a result, they asked for help more easily the next day. Although in the beginning not all teams achieved their goals, Rob did not get angry but facilitated the search for solutions.

Looking back, Rob managed to change the culture by starting two new habits. First, helping each other complete the work for the day became normal after a few weeks and was therefore incorporated relatively quickly. Second was the habit of thinking in terms of solutions and possibilities. Before Rob came, it was customary to cover up mistakes, to not find fault with yourself, and to not improve. Now, discovered errors were seen as opportunities for improvement. They were made concrete and then quickly fixed in small steps. Because employees really noticed the improvements, slowly confidence arose that things would really change. Rob took accountability because he himself wanted to set the example. He had asked various employees for feedback about what he could improve. When employees came up with feedback and ideas, he checked back later to ask whether they noticed change. In this way, he inspired others to be vulnerable and ask for feedback.

Thanks to these two new habits, there was a new culture in the department of helping each other, sharing knowledge, achieving daily results together, feeling responsible for dossiers, giving personal feedback, continuously increasing quality, and asking for help. This increased customer satisfaction by more than 30 points and employee satisfaction from a low 6 to a steady 8.

Rob slowly turns away from the window. He grabs his bag and greets the last team members who are still working. As he walks out, he wonders how he can further anchor the new culture—because it doesn't feel like a steady and stable culture yet.

How Do You Improve the Culture?

So far, this book has covered mostly pretty tangible topics like goals, ownership, customer impact, learning faster, and the skills that go alongside. As stated in the beginning of this book, the responsibility of the agile leader is to create an environment for the teams to thrive. This means an environment in which they can take ownership (Part 2) on tangible goals (Part 1) and learn quickly from customer feedback (Part 3). A first step in creating this environment is to start using the tools already explained. A next step is to improve the culture in which the teams operate.

For a successful change to agile, it is crucial that the culture fits with the agile way of working. The culture must promote learning, transparency, candor, collaboration, and customer focus. A local culture without these aspects will likely lose its agility. Improving the culture is hard and takes time but is nevertheless crucial. In recent years I have been looking for relatively simple and effective ways to improve the culture of a team or department. The leader can influence the local culture within the scope of his mandate or responsibility. It's of course harder to influence the culture outside the direct mandate of the leader; the latter is not part of this section. In this final part, I'll give several practical ways to influence and improve the local culture.

Seeking ways to improve culture, I interviewed several leaders, looked back on successful changes, and brainstormed with managers. This showed that several successful leaders were unconsciously skilled at changing the culture. Studying them and interviewing them revealed that, at first, they didn't really understand why they were often able to change the local culture. But along the way we discovered that they had a keen eye for two things. First, culture follows structure[1] (Larman's law). That's why the first and biggest part of the leadership toolkit in this book is to give new structures, new tools, new metrics, and new meetings. Second, they were unconsciously skilled in changing habits and in influencing heroes (informal leaders). They saw habits that strongly influenced the culture. Next, they had an eye for the informal leaders and how they anchored a culture. Let's have a closer look.

1. http://www.craiglarman.com/wiki/index.php?title=Larman%27s_Laws_of_Organizational_Behavior

Improving culture is a tough and intensive process that requires perseverance and vision. Culture has all sorts of facets and ingredients that intervene and work together.

- **Language, jargon.** Specific words and slang that have a meaning and create a group feeling. New people need to start to learn these words before they can be effective in the system.
- **Habits; "That's how we do it here."** Ingrained behaviors that are common. People who don't do these behaviors are perceived as weird or at least different.
- **Heroes or informal leaders.** People who are respected and followed because of their achievements for the whole group. Their behavior is copied.
- **History.** Behavior of previous managers, mergers.
- **Symbols, reports.** Overviews, icons, flags, or lists that define the group.
- **Norms and values.** The values that drive the behavior; for example, caring for the poor, taking care of the world's environment, green energy, abiding tax laws, or smaller things like being on time for a meeting, starting a meeting with a social talk, or the level of formality with which emails are written.

These ingredients influence each other and together form the culture. This makes culture very complex and sticky. Together they form a system of "ingredients" that intervene and influence each other. (For further details on system thinking, take a look at the work of Peter Senge.) Changing the system of intervening and influencing ingredients is difficult for two reasons. First, each ingredient can't be studied by itself without the relation to the other ingredients. Next, one person can't have an overview of the whole system; it's too complex and therefore requires different perspectives. Luckily, that doesn't mean that culture is fixed and impossible to change. The solution is to start with one or two ingredients while having the perspective on the whole by using the views and experiences of different people.

Based on my experience over the past years, a good practice to improve the culture is by focusing primarily on three ingredients, namely, *habits* first, and after that *symbols* and *heroes*. By first changing the habits (the routine behavior) and then adding better symbols (reports, overviews, lists), a culture change is started. After that, new heroes or new informal leaders are needed to really anchor the culture.

So how do you improve the culture? It consists of the following (iterative) steps. For each improvement you want to make in the culture, these four steps can be used.

1. Discover a part of the culture you want to improve.
2. Together with a few people, brainstorm on the habits that drive the existing culture.
3. Discover new, healthy habits that drive the desired change.
4. Anchor the change by adjusting symbols (reports, overviews, lists) and guiding informal leaders to show the right behavior.

These steps are also the sequence of the rest of this part of the book. These steps will change the culture, not with a big-bang change, but with many small iterations. These four steps can be used for a single improvement or for several improvements simultaneously. Successful agile leaders continuously improve the culture to improve the inspirational environment for their teams. Healthy culture is crucial for thriving self-managing teams. The culture is—as it were—the oxygen for the team. Without it, for example, collaboration is impossible and teams are not effectively focused on customer impact. Leaders can't micromanage or control their teams. They are, however, crucial in creating and improving the culture. Because, as I will explain about informal leaders, self-managing teams can't fix bad informal leaders themselves. They need the formal leader to step in and fix it.

To focus on a cultural improvement topic, let's have a closer look at what an agile culture actually is.

What Is an Agile Culture?

As mentioned previously, it's important that the culture also matches the agile way of working.

- The results of the team are more important than the individual results of an employee.
- Compliments and appreciation of customers and users are the real proof of success.
- Employees with different disciplines exchange knowledge and experience.
- There is continuous innovation through experiments.
- Team thinking is crucial; no single employee can see the big picture by himself.
- In the event of mistakes, it is stated in a fair and transparent way what went wrong so that many can learn from it.
- The informal heroes are those employees who let teams win and others grow.
- Stopping projects, products, or ideas prematurely is not a failure but a celebration because something has been learned.
- Helping customers is more important than following internal processes and procedures.

Brainstorming with several people on these aspects of an agile culture is a good starting point to find a first cultural improvement. If the current culture of an organization is the opposite of the previous description of an agile culture, the agile method will probably never grow nor thrive.

With this first cultural improvement identified, let's have a closer look at how habits influence the culture and how habits can be changed.

WHY DID THE EXISTING HABITS BLOCK THE NEW CULTURE?

Before Rob started changing, there were a few strong habits in his department. The first is the habit around the "work stock," or backlog. The work stock of an individual employee was so high that he could not finish the work within a few days. The habit was to not ask for help and to just go home at the end of the day. Suppose that some people tried to change the habit and ask for help. And others started to help out. The people who helped couldn't finish their own work or else they would look bad on the individual metrics. That isn't a reward for new behavior, so it will never become a habit or culture to help others. Suppose that Rob had organized an energizing event "today inside, today outside" with all kinds of motivational speakers, culture workshops, and other inspiration sessions. Would this have had a long-term effect? Probably not, because an employee can hardly solve a problem on his own. The existing structure blocked the new culture.

What Are Habits?

A habit[2] is an act or behavior that one is accustomed to and one does not think about explicitly. Think of brushing your teeth, stopping for red light, rolling your shoulders when you are tense, or taking off your shoes when you come home. A habit consists of three steps: trigger, routine, and reward. The habit is triggered, after which the routine is rewarded. Together these three parts form the habit loop (see Figure 4.1).

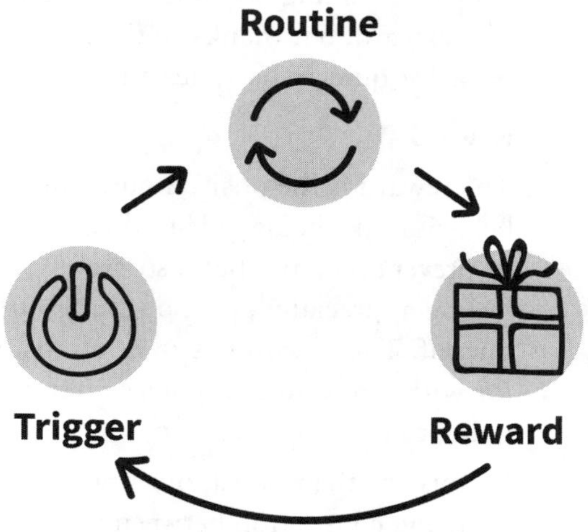

Figure 4.1 The habit loop

2. https://www.merriam-webster.com/dictionary/habit

Let's have a closer look at the three parts of this habit loop.

Trigger

The trigger is a situation, moment, or event. This trigger initiates a reaction from a person or a team. It's like pressing a button that turns the habit on. Thanks to earlier (positive) experiences, the mental behavior is shaped. Without much thinking or reconsidering, previous action or behavior is initiated.

Routine

The routine is the behavior or action that might have been uncomfortable at first but is becoming more and more familiar. From opening a door to giving feedback, covering mistakes, working harder, or even experiencing emotions like getting stressed, feeling happy, or smiling. At first the behavior might feel new or awkward, but thanks to the positive reward, the behavior quickly becomes a routine.

Reward

The reward is the positive outcome or benefit of the behavior, like being able to do something more easily or preventing pain, but also more vague things like feeling appreciated, part of the group, or better about oneself. The reward has to be almost instant. A behavior with a reward that comes after a few days isn't going to be a routine.

Because of the reward, our brains make an increasingly strong connection between the trigger and the action, until in time we act without thinking about it.

How Do Habits Change?

How do the old and new habits fit into the habit loop?

Habit 1: Own Stock

Table 4.1 Own stock

	Old Habit	New Habit
Trigger 	During the day, the employee looks at his own stock of work.	
Routine 	He sees the large work stock. He spends the rest of the afternoon doing his best, but it does not get done in one day. He does not ask for help.	He sees the work stock, but it is too big to be completely eliminated this afternoon. He consults with the team and asks other teams for help.
Reward 	No negative feeling. Has the same work stock as other employees. Nobody asks for help.	Team feeling. Work stock is zero at the end of the day. Satisfied feeling that the work is completed. Go home on time.

In order to realize the change—to ask for help—the new behavior of an employee must be rewarded in the short term, almost instantly. If the employee, for example, gets help and besides feeling part of the team also can finish his own stock of work for today, it's more likely this behavior becomes a routine (see Table 4.1). But in the current environment, asking for help would not work because everyone is busy. If somebody gives help, that person will have an even higher pile of work; so probably, nobody offers help. Working longer as well does not help because it concerns a structural problem. People might work longer for a few days, but that doesn't become a routine because the pile of work remains high. So because no alternative behavior has a short-term positive reward, nobody can change the habit and thus the culture at the individual level. That is why the current habit is such a strong part of the existing culture. The agile leader has to change the environment first before the new behavior can thrive—and only after the new behavior is felt positively in the short term. This allows the new behavior and habits of employees to transform the culture.

Habit 2: Something Goes Wrong

Table 4.2 illustrates what happens when something goes wrong.

Table 4.2 What happens when something goes wrong

	Old Habit	New Habit
Trigger 	A mistake is discovered.	
Routine 	Blame others. Point to others that caused the mistake.	Brainstorm together with different people on the root cause and possible solutions. Learn from the mistake and improve.
Reward 	No negative attention. No need to change. Focus on own work.	Team spirit. Improvements are really implemented. The number of mistakes lowers. There are more satisfied customers.

As soon as a mistake or an error occurred, the previous managers searched for what had gone wrong. See Table 4.2 for the habit loop of this example. The “guilty” got—so to speak—a slap on the wrist. Because the learning wasn’t shared with others, similar errors were not prevented. Employees who shared their mistakes openly received negative attention from the managers. And employees who took the time to implement improvements increased the debt in their own workload, which was not appreciated by the former executives. As a result, this habit couldn’t be changed at the employee level because there was no substitute behavior that was rewarded in the short term.

Only when Rob regularly held discussions with various employees to improve things and made these improvements really visible and tangible did the new habit slowly arise. Rob also set a good example by sharing his own mistakes at departmental meetings with a good dose of humor.

It can be concluded that habits are an important instrument for cultural change. In doing so, the agile leader acts, as it were, as a habit architect: he designs new habits that change the culture positively. In the following sections I will discuss two practical tools that help to improve a culture: the Habit Matrix and the TO-GRIP pattern.

How Quickly Are Habits Copied?

The stronger the culture, the faster the daily habits are copied by new employees. If the custom is to make coffee for each other, new employees will copy that within a day and thereby strengthen the culture. The same applies to the habit of going home around 5 p.m., regardless of whether the work is finished for that day. New employees who stay later to finish their work in the beginning and who are barely rewarded by their environment often stop doing so.

In the TV series *Brain Games*, National Geographic showed a wonderful study of how fast habits become part of the culture of a group. Search YouTube for "Brain Games Peer Pressure," a movie of about 4.5 minutes. Here you see a woman enter a waiting room. With a beep sound, everyone in the waiting room stands up. How long would it take before she got up like the others? Exactly three beeps. Would she also continue to stand up if there is nobody else in the waiting room? Would she transfer the behavior to a new group? In the video, you finally see a completely new group with waiting people standing up at the beep. Here is a clear habitual loop. The trigger is the sound, the routine is getting up, and the reward is "belonging." The group pressure ensures that a new habit is quickly adopted.

4.2 HOW DO YOU DESIGN HEALTHY HABITS?

Leaders give the right example, even if nobody is watching.

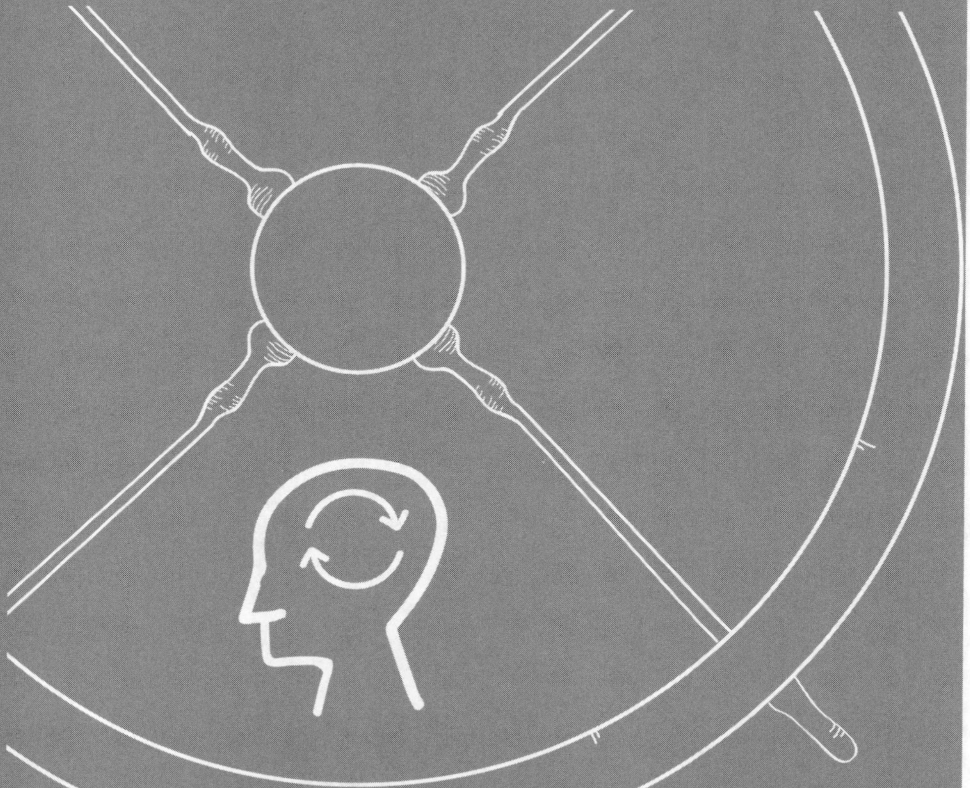

Introduction Questions

1. What habits in your organization contribute to the agile culture? Why?
2. Which unhealthy habits have you been trying to stop for a while?

Improving culture starts with improving habits. Luckily, habits that already contribute to the agile culture need not be changed. But habits that break down the agile culture must be tackled; these are the unhealthy habits. How does an agile leader recognize habits that do not contribute to the agile culture? How does he recognize habits that are destroying collaboration, blocking continuous improvement, and preventing the team from being agile?

There are two steps to explain how unhealthy habits can be found. First, the leader has to understand how unhealthy habits work, and second, he has to use the brainpower of different people to brainstorm on the root cause of undesired effects.

Healthy and Unhealthy Habits

The first step to understanding how the habits that don't contribute to the agile culture can be found is to know how unhealthy habits work. Unhealthy habits are unfortunately difficult to recognize in practice. As seen in the habit loop, the short-term reward of any habit is positive. Therefore, the distinction can only be found in the long term. This gives the key to finding unhealthy habits: by deliberately searching for negative long-term consequences. Table 4.3 shows habits with different short-term incentives and long-term effects.

To prevent this long-term negative effect, we sometimes forbid certain behavior or act differently purely based on discipline. Knowing how habits work, this doesn't change the underlying natural behavior. When the control or punishment lowers, or during a moment of weakness, the underlying habit emerges back. This happens because changing the underlying habit requires a short-term positive reward. Table 4.3 summarizes these relationships.

Table 4.3 Relationship among healthy and unhealthy habits and discipline

	Healthy Habit	**Unhealthy Habit**	**No Habit. Discipline**
Reward	Positive	Positive	Negative
Long-term effect	Positive	Negative	Positive

To illustrate a personal example about unhealthy habits, as a manager, I had the habit of giving answers to every question that my direct reports asked me. That's because I was the leader who also had the technical knowledge. There was a direct short-term reward of this routine because the people got a good answer (or so it seemed at first) and it gave me good feeling of being needed and being smart. But the long-term downside was that I didn't teach my people to find answers themselves, and at times the answers that I gave weren't good enough because I didn't know all the details of the problem. Ignoring the questions or not giving an answer at all didn't work either because that gave both the direct report and me a negative reward. Giving them the answer "You can figure this out yourself" was (in hindsight) purely based on discipline because that also didn't give me the feeling of being needed (nor being smart). Looking at the nature of habits, I had to find a new behavior that would give me a positive short-term reward and a positive long-term effect. So what would that be? Let's put this example in a matrix (Table 4.4).

Table 4.4 Matrix

	Unhealthy Habit	**Discipline**
Trigger	People ask me all kinds of questions and I think I know the answer.	
Routine	Answer	Say, "You can figure this out yourself."
Reward	☺ Feel needed. People happy with good answer (so it seemed).	☹ Don't feel needed. People not happy because they already tried to find out themselves.
Effect	☹ A lot of questions. Not learning to find answers.	☹ More problems unsolved and people didn't grow that much.

So, looking at the matrix, it seems that I have to find a new behavior that would be positive both in the short term and in the long term. I tried several things, and after talking to a coach I found the (relatively simple) solution to coach and mentor the person to find the answer. For example, I tried the two things outlined in Table 4.5.

Table 4.5 Alternatives

	Alternative 1: Mentor	**Alternative 2: Learning Culture**
Trigger	People ask me all kinds of questions and I think I know the answer.	
Routine	Say, "What did you already do? Let's use that to find new solutions."	Say, "Let's put the answer also in forum or knowledge base" (KB).
Reward	☺ Feel needed. People happy with even better answer (so it seemed).	☺ Feel needed. Reviewed the answer in the KB or forum so it was properly recorded.
Effect	☺ For simple questions, they could find the answers themselves, which saved me time. And for the harder ones, we did it together.	☺ Others saw the value of the KB and start to use it also. Slowly this helped in changing to a learning and sharing culture.

The preceding matrices are the basis of a new tool called the Habit Matrix. This is Tool 7 of this book and the first tool of Part 4.

TOOL 7: HABIT MATRIX

Unfortunately, it is often impossible to see directly the consequences of one's habit towards the culture. This is because the routine has a short-term positive reward but a long-term negative effect on the culture. So how can the unhealthy habits be found? It works better to study the undesired long-term effects first and use a group of people to discover or unveil the underlying unhealthy habits. I have developed a tool to help agile leaders in this process: the Habit Matrix. This tool supports the agile leader in a culture workshop. The purpose of this workshop is to find undesirable effects and underlying unhealthy habits and help to design healthy habits together. The Habit Matrix is illustrated in Figure 4.2.

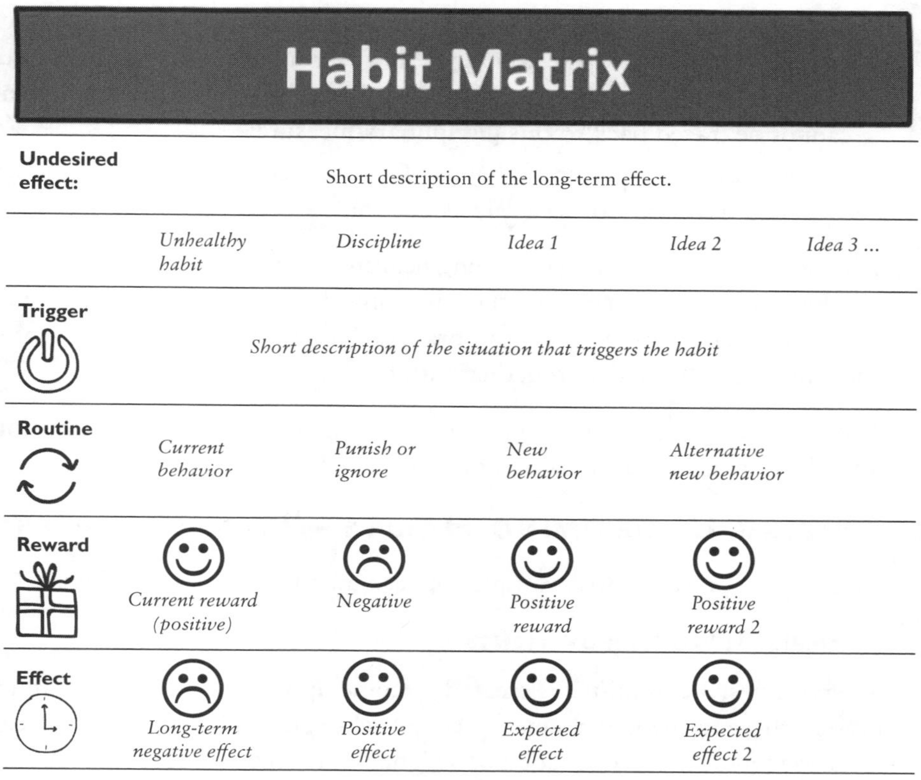
Habit Matrix
Undesired effect:
Short description of the long-term effect.
Unhealthy habit
Discipline
Idea 1
Idea 2
Idea 3 ...
Trigger
Short description of the situation that triggers the habit
Routine
Current behavior
Punish or ignore
New behavior
Alternative new behavior
Reward
Current reward (positive)
Negative
Positive reward
Positive reward 2
Effect
Long-term negative effect
Positive effect
Expected effect
Expected effect 2

Figure 4.2 The Habit Matrix

By consecutively following the next steps, the Habit Matrix can be filled in.

1. Describe the current unwanted effect.
2. Describe in a very concrete way an exemplary situation that triggers the habit. It is important to make this as specific as possible. Do not write something like "I see apple pie," but rather, describe the moment, situation, feeling, or environment.
3. Then describe the current routine.
4. Describe the direct reward. This step is important in order to ultimately design a good new habit. The good description of the reward usually fails on the first attempt. It helps to spend time asking questions and working together to make the direct reward specific. In the example of the apple pie, the reward is not a filled stomach or eaten pie, but good taste, relaxation, energy break, and enjoyment.

5. Make the discipline explicit. This is the act based on willpower without positive reward. Make the (negative) short-term incentive of doing nothing or taking a concrete disciplinary action. Then the long-term effect often cannot be traced back to this disciplinary measure.
6. Brainstorm about alternative habits. Try to match the current routine with the short-term reward as closely as possible.

The most important key to designing healthy habits is to find new behavior that has almost the same short-term incentive but now has a positive long-term effect. This is often collective brainstorming, searching, experimenting, and exploring alternatives together with others.

The next sections contain some concrete examples of both the recognition of underlying habits and the design of healthy habits.

Recognizing Underlying Habits—Two Examples

This section presents two examples of recognizing underlying habits.

Example 1: No Improvements

Several times, a committee is created to come up with improvements and to present these to the management. After a while, it can be seen that no real improvements have been made. Why? The improvements were tangible, were concrete, and had a clear benefit. From the perspective of finding the unhealthy habit, new insight emerges. One habit strongly causes the lack of real improvements. When, during the workday, the manager sees that the workload can't be finished, he asks the employees to work harder to reach the schedule of that day. This triggers the routine to just work harder and focus on the short-term workload. On a daily basis, the employees are primarily rewarded on what they have produced on that day. As a result, the employees close the day and the week with a largely satisfied feeling. The employees who have done extra receive the appreciation of colleagues for this.

The routine that the agile leader has to create is this: if the production lags behind, we will not work harder anymore. The employee who does make improvements and thus obtains lower numbers is appreciated. This routine can't be changed on the employee level. The agile leader can't ask his employees to self-manage this problem. He has to change the system to change the culture. Let's have a look at the Habit Matrix from the perspective of the employee (Table 4.6).

Table 4.6 Habit Matrix: No improvements

Undesired effect:	There are ideas for improvements but these are not implemented. There is no culture of continuous learning and improvement.			
	Unhealthy Habit	**Discipline**	**Idea 1**	**Idea 2**
Trigger		Running behind on a daily schedule		
Routine	Work harder and/or longer.	Just stop at 5 o'clock.	Schedule improvement.	Improve use of days off.
Reward	☺ Reached the target and the schedule.	☹ Unsatisfied customer and manager.	☺ Reached the target and the schedule.	☺ Implemented improvements.
Effect	☹ Quick fix, no improvements. Drained. Same song every day.	☺ At home in time, but no improvements.	☺ Solid and long-term fixes. Effective.	☺ Long-term fixes. Culture of improvements.

The employee really wants to implement improvements. But under the current system, the structure doesn't reward him for spending time on it. Only when the pressure is lowered and the focus on short-term output is reduced can the employees start implementing improvements. The agile leader has to create room for the new habits by changing the system. He architects new habits by changing the environment and creating a short-term reward for new behavior. This new behavior can settle in and become part of the new culture.

Example 2: No Team Players

After the agile way of working is implemented, there are several team members that didn't become team players. Take, for example, Matthew. He has been working for the company for more than 20 years. Several people have complained about his ego in recent months. Matthew thinks his own work is more important than the work for the team. He achieves more on his own than with the team, he says often. Other managers come directly to

Matthew with customer complaints or critical bugs. Matthew then leaves his team and quickly saves the company. Many executives and customers value Matthew for his rapid analysis and solution skills. He gets a pat on the back, and colleagues from other departments thank him for his quick performance.

The unhealthy habit that the agile leader has to break is, when it really matters, we are used to asking an individual. This creates the impression that, when the heat is on, the team is less important than an individual team member. This creates no team culture and no cooperation. What does Matthew's Habit Matrix look like? What are new behaviors that could flourish in the agile culture? Review Table 4.7.

Table 4.7 Habit Matrix: No team players

Undesired effect:	Senior employees are not team players but are individual "firefighters."			
	Unhealthy Habit	**Discipline**	**Idea 1**	**Idea 2**
Trigger	Customer complaint or critical bug			
Routine	Matthew the firefighter fixes it.	Matthew is forbidden to solely help.	The reserved time is spent to fix and structurally solve.	Together with a mentee, Matthew can fix the solution.
Reward	☺ Pat on the back. Savior. Seen as expert.	☹ Slower solution. Demotivated Matthew.	☺ Also solve the structural solution within the team as a team.	☺ Knowledge transfer on the job. Together, structurally solved.
Effect	☹ Quick fix, no improvements.	😐 Some knowledge transfer. Matthew is less unique.	☺ Matthew is seen as the mentor and driver for structural solutions.	☺ Long-term fixes. Knowledge transfer.

One of the reasons the way things have been done is a strong habit is because the reward is totally for Matthew and the real negative effect is for others. Matthew hardly has any negative (long-term) effect for his firefighter job. Because of the status of Matthew in the rest of the organization, he is the informal leader or hero of the team. Because of group dynamics, the team can't fix this by just relying on "self-managing power." The agile leader has to step in and change the system and the hero status. We'll have more on these group dynamics and the hero topic in the next section.

Role of the Agile Leader

It can be concluded that replacing unhealthy habits with new healthy habits is a good way to change the culture. The role of the agile leader is that of the habit architect. For this, he must become skilled in recognizing unhealthy habits that are the cause of unwanted cultural effects, situations, or results. Then he can—together with others—replace this unhealthy habit with healthy habits that do contribute to an agile culture. It is important that the agile leader guards the culture, especially when there is pressure or stress. Because if, under pressure from disappointing results, short-term incentives of good behavior are not met, collaboration, long-term investment, and mutual learning will be postponed. This is automatically the moment when unhealthy habits can quickly take root. The carefully constructed and costly agile culture can crumble.

So, in the four steps of changing the culture, there is 1) a concrete improvement and 2) the underlying unhealthy habit is found. Step 3 is to design healthy habits. And last but not least, Step 4 is to anchor the change by aligning it with the symbols and the heroes. Let's have a closer look.

Two Cultural Leaders

Mahatma Gandhi created a revolution in the early 1900s. He called on people to protest nonviolently against the apartheid and oppression of Indians. He was thus a leader of a new culture. He set people in motion not to opt for violence, and therefore only the short-term effect, but to work precisely for the long-term effect. He inspired people to go for the real long-lasting change, at any price.

Nelson Mandela was also a leader of a new culture. He is acclaimed worldwide for his influence in creating the new South Africa, and he received the Nobel Peace Prize for this work. During his long prison term from 1964 to 1982, he began to empathize with the different population groups. He saw that the whites were keeping the other population groups under control because they were afraid of a genocide. This fear strengthened apartheid. Mandela could be the new leader because he could really empathize with the needs, fears, and thoughts of others. He understood why people behaved in a certain way and what motivated the leaders. As a result, he could later bridge the cultural differences as president. He inspired and motivated people not to go for the short-term results, but to address the pain and go for the long-term benefit. Through it all, he was a personal example.

4.3 CAN YOU ANCHOR THE CULTURAL IMPROVEMENT?

We are what we repeatedly do. Excellence then, is not an act, but a habit.

– Will Durant

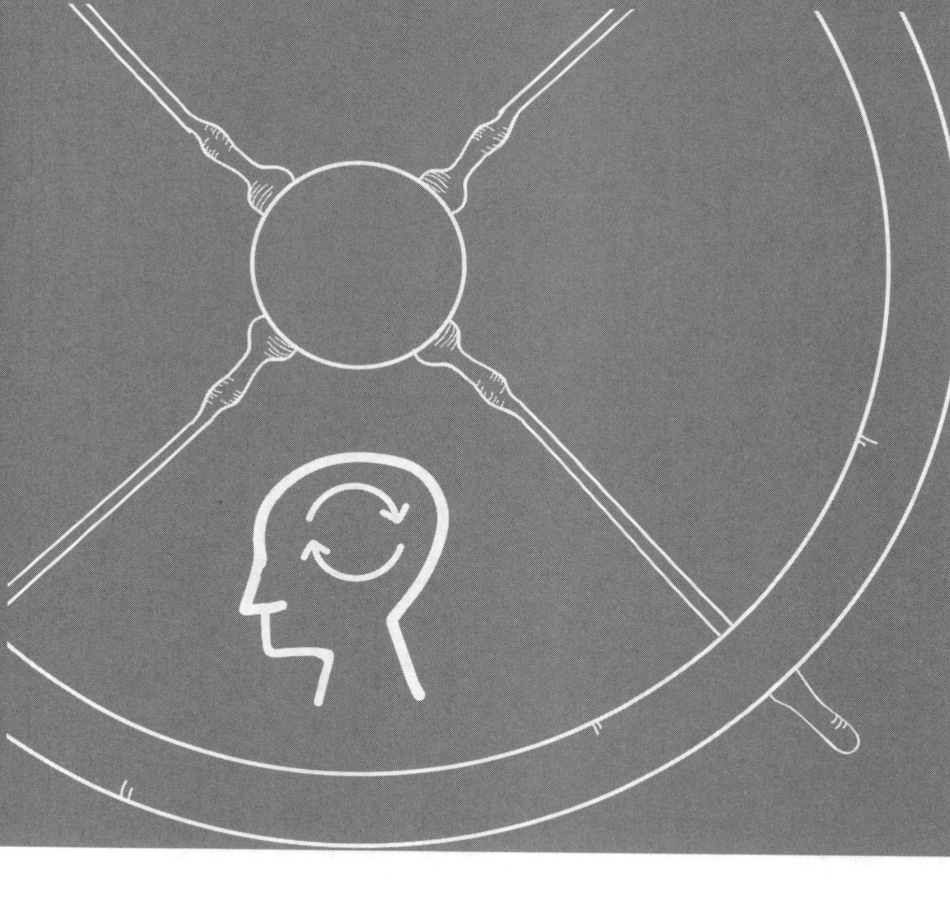

Introduction Questions

Design healthy **HABITS**

1. Who are the heroes in your organization? Are they driving and supporting the healthy culture?
2. Which heroes are a personal example of the desired culture?

Introduction

Mike opened the sales meeting on Monday morning at 9 a.m. He had been the director for years but wanted to sail a new course. The company still had good earnings on existing market segments and its top three products. To be future-proof, however, new market segments had to be tapped, and other products needed to be sold. Mike knew for years that two top sellers were the heroes of the company. These two pulled in very large orders that contributed largely to the success of the company. The employees who wanted to sell the new and innovative products had to put more effort into smaller orders and therefore did not stand out even though they did build on the future of the organization, and in contrast to the two top sellers, were busy with new markets to tap or new products to make.

Mike had to change something. At first, he successfully introduced new habits: working together much more, bringing clients together, and sharing knowledge. However, that did not yet sufficiently bring about the desired change. It was time for his heroes to change, or it was time to get new heroes.

It took a while before Mike realized that the reports, the bonuses, and the promotional rules in his organization determined who the formal heroes were. He had started to call these drivers *symbols*. Mike suspected that the reports had to be changed first. From then on, he showed orders in a different order: it was not the size of the order that was decisive, but whether it concerned orders of innovative products. Suddenly, other orders were at the top and other employees could tell what they had done to get these products to sell. These employees received more attention and appreciation. Mike repeatedly emphasized why the new reporting overview was important for the future of the company.

After a few weeks, Mike noticed that heroes started to change. The two top sellers adjusted their behavior and started to sell innovative and not-so-big deals. They became the heroes of the new-way mindset. Those who did not want to change initially received hardly any attention. And if they did not want to change after a while, a lively conversation with Mike awaited. Fortunately, some heroes also received all of the rewards from other employees, making them the new informal leaders. This created the real change.

Who Are the Heroes of an Agile Culture?

The heroes or informal leaders of an agile culture are those people who are successful with their attitude and behavior, and their behavior is copied by others. They have so-called followers who also want to be successful and therefore copy the behavior. Heroes could have a positive or a negative contribution to the culture. When, for example, a person cheats, lies, and doesn't help others but his behavior makes him successful and he is not corrected by the formal leader, his behavior is likely to be copied by others. And this disintegrates the culture. When a new person joins or steps up and he is successful by showing the opposite behavior and is being honest, vulnerable, and a real team player, that person can kind of fight the existing hero and get the informal leader status from the group. Then he can drive the new culture and, after a while, a total different vibe and atmosphere can emerge.

Because heroes need to be successful, a hero's status is supported by the symbols like reports, lists, overviews, and bonuses. Because they are so successful and their behavior is copied by others, their behavior is resilient. It's likely that they will show the same behavior repeatedly. This makes them the anchors of the culture. The heroes get their status from basic group dynamics—from the interaction between the people in the group. Because their mindset is copied and their behavior is followed by others, they retrieve the hero status. They have an informal influence on their environment.

To see why the existing culture is so hard to change and to anchor the new behavior in the culture, the agile leader has to develop a keen eye for these heroes. Successful agile leaders have a clear and concrete picture of what they expect from influencing people. The more concrete and tangible this image is, the easier he can recognize, appreciate, and support the right people. Guiding these heroes to the new way of working is in fact a very effective way of driving change. It's not a change with a thick approach, milestones, and a lot of pressure and power. No, it's the total opposite: a viral change. It's a change that is ignited and self-spreads throughout the teams.

These informal leaders will be an example for the rest and will take the rest into the change. It can be concluded that the culture is anchored when the symbols and heroes are aligned. For that, it is important that the reports, overviews, and promotions stimulate the right heroes.

A Few People Define the Culture for Many

Looking at the culture through the paradigm of heroes creates a different perspective of cultural change. The agile leader has to focus only on a few heroes to change the culture of many. When these heroes show the new behavior, live the new habits, and provide personal examples of the agile culture, they will influence the rest. This creates a whole new mindset for the actual change. The agile leader starts a fire by influencing the right few heroes who will then influence the rest. This immediately emphasizes the importance of having the right heroes in the organization. When a wrong hero is influencing other people, the agile culture can't thrive.

From group-dynamics perspective, the rest of the employees will have an almost impossible job to influence the wrong hero. This is the role and responsibility of the agile leader. He has to step in and take action. Often it drills down to two options:

- Influence and convince the hero to change, or
- Take hard measures and ultimately, if needed, fire the heroes who have a bad influence on the culture.

How Do You Anchor the Cultural Improvement?

After finding a cultural improvement, discovering the unhealthy habits, and designing new healthy habits to replace them, the last but not least step is to anchor the cultural improvement. Consider the following steps to really change the culture.

1. Change the symbols of the organization to promote the agile behavior. The symbols are things like reports, overviews, rules for promotion, and bonuses. If these symbols promote short-term thinking, such as working harder, not sharing knowledge, and covering mistakes, then these symbols decide who the heroes are. On the other hand, if symbols promote long-term goals, such as working together and working toward one goal, then agile heroes will thrive.

2. Spot the heroes. Who are rewarded or followed by the rest? Whose behavior is copied? Talk with these people one on one to understand their motivation, their passion, and their talents.
3. Talk openly with the group about what we expect from each other. Create a clear image of good behavior.
4. Make heroes successful with the new behavior, mindset, and attitude. This can be accomplished by mentoring existing heroes to adapt or by mentoring new heroes to stand up.
5. If needed, take drastic measures toward the wrong heroes. These are the weeds between the crops.

It can be concluded that informal leaders emerge or change by changing the symbols and at the same time coaching them during the change. In addition, these informal influencing people have the chance to change their colleagues. If they succeed in being an example to the rest with their new attitude and behavior, the agile culture can become a reality.

Now one more thing is important: the habits of the agile leader himself around the implementation of improvements and strategic points. How can an agile leader learn the good habits about decisions, improvements, setting goals, and giving direction—in other words, the habits that belong in an agile culture? In the next section, I'll give a practical tool for this.

4.4 WHAT IS A HEALTHY HABIT TO IMPLEMENT IMPROVEMENTS?

In a complex environment, improvements can't be planned or budgeted.

Improvements are explored step by step.

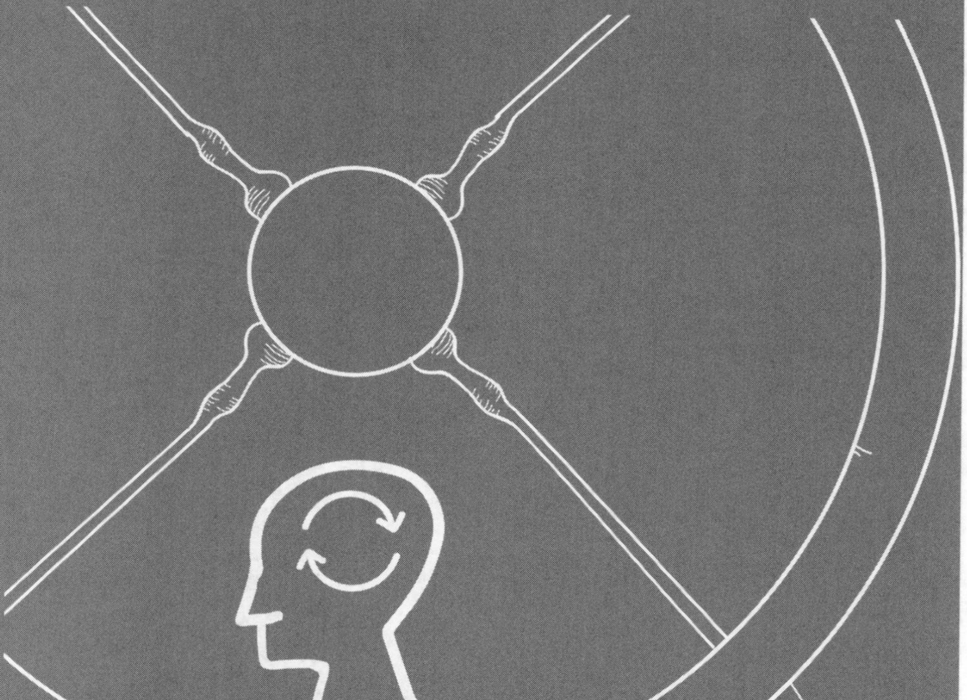

Introduction Questions

1. How are strategic improvements implemented in your organization?
2. Which strategic improvements are so complex and unpredictable that they cannot be planned?

Introduction

Being almost at the end of this practical book, let's have a look again at David, the person I mentioned in the introduction. He has been an agile leader for over 9 months, and he is very happy with the successful changes that have taken place over the past months. He feels that he has overcome the most difficult period. He now knows how to set goals that increase the focus on the customer. He also sees that teams now take ownership because they get the right freedom. They continuously grow and develop initiatives. Fortunately, the teams now learn much faster from customers, so they know much better if they are doing well.

David phoned me. He is still struggling with one last important question. A few local improvements are so great that they have to be implemented across multiple teams. The teams can very well implement improvements that are directly related to their own focus and customer impact. But making large changes across multiple teams is still hard and, so far, unsuccessful. For example, the complete customer journey needs to be improved. The quality of the software code must also increase, and another improvement concerns the laws and regulations that are mandatory with a fixed deadline. Several teams must work together for this. David had the personal habit of making these analyses himself, drafting plans and making budgets available. If he would do that again, he would break the carefully constructed agile culture again. He foresees that the teams would see this as command and control, and as a result they would not learn to handle improvements themselves, they wouldn't pick ownership on these topics, and he would have to focus too much on the details instead of on improving the environment.

David knows that the change starts with him. He wants to teach himself a new habit to make major improvements and changes. Only then can he expect this from the employees themselves. But what is a good habit for this? For this, David wants to implement these big improvements in such a way that it strengthens the culture of collaboration, experimentation, and learning from the customers. He has an idea: the principles of continuous learning, making things measurable, and applying fast adjustments also apply to these major improvements and changes. He asks for my support during the implementation. Together we discovered the final tool of this book: TO-GRIP.

Enabling Improvements

The agile leader is responsible for adapting and improving the environment of the self-managing teams so the teams can grow. Teams have the natural tendency to grow like crops in a field. When crops don't grow well, the farmer adapts the environment until the crops thrive.

After implementing the tools already described, the teams have an inspirational direction; they take ownership over the products and services, and they learn quickly from users to continuously improve. But how can the agile leader improve the continuous-improvement culture? Without this culture, the current level of performance is likely to be ingrained while the world around is accelerating. These two don't match. The leader can (traditionally) decide to push the teams and set ambitious targets, but that's not improving the culture either. The leader can just wait for his teams to step up and improve, but what if that takes too long or just isn't good enough? How can the leader use the culture of self-managing teams?

It would be even greater if this also would give a certain level of control over the improvement, making it clear where we currently are with the improvement and what is likely to be done next.

How do teams learn from each other? Self-managing teams don't learn through a fixed, up-front program. That's too traditional but also fundamentally impossible because the new improvement has yet to be explored and unveiled. There is no map or quick solution to find these improvements. These teams learn through social learning. And big change and improvements go viral. There are three basic ingredients needed to drive viral change. They are partly derived from the work of Leandro Herrero.[3]

1. A relatively small group of people can have a great power in the creation of change.
2. The formal leaders and structure have to support this small group of change enablers.
3. The first steps of change should be quickly beneficial and rewarding.

Over the past years, millions of people have quickly adapted their behavior and copied the behavior of others. From Angry Birds and Pokémon GO to Facebook and the use of smartphones for things other than calling somebody—most of them have these three basic ingredients ingrained in their success.

3. https://leandroherrero.com/the-key-viral-change-principles/

Relatively Small Group

The small group that has great power in the creation of change first includes the few people who initiated the idea. For Angry Birds, the characters and game concept were created by a man named Jaakko Iisalo from Finland.[4] Together with a small group of people, he worked on the prototype and launched the first game. Now millions of people play the game on a daily basis. Pokémon GO was launched in 2016, and the team of builders had great power in the creation of change: as of May 2018, the game had been downloaded over 800 million times.[5]

Support

The success of Angry Birds and Facebook are made possible thanks to a lot of things, from mobile internet infrastructure to all the technologies needed in the smartphones. Thirty years ago, these changes were impossible because there was no underlying support.

First Steps

Games like Pokémon GO and apps like Facebook purposefully design the gameplay and ease of use, respectively, within the first few minutes. The first levels of Angry Birds are very easy, and the user feels like he can do it. Netflix states that users should have a new movie picked within 60 to 90 seconds,[6] otherwise they could lose interest and move to something else. Therefore, the first steps of the new behavior should be easy and quickly rewarding.

So, how could these insights on social change be used in companies to drive change within the teams?

Tool 8: TO-GRIP

In recent years, I have seen many leaders wrestle with the implementation of major improvement programs. They looked for ways other than carrying out analysis, planning, and managing costs. For this there is a practical tool for the

4. https://www.theguardian.com/artanddesign/2016/feb/23/how-we-made-angry-birds
5. https://www.pocketgamer.biz/news/68209/pokemon-go-captures-800-million-downloads/
6. https://www.businessinsider.com/how-long-netflix-thinks-it-takes-to-choose-content-2016-2

agile leader: TO-GRIP. This tool supports brainstorming and continuous improvement. TO-GRIP thus supports the agile leader in creating an environment in which different teams implement major improvements together.

TO-GRIP, the eighth tool in this book, consists of six parts that can be defined and made into a concise story (see Figure 4.3). Every part is important for the tool to work properly. At the start, not all the parts have to be in place; these parts could be filled in after a few days or weeks. The tool is based on the idea of social or viral change, in which change or improvements are initiated by a few and copied by others. It can be used for improvements, strategic points, or major changes. Both agile leaders as team members or informal leaders can take the initiative to use this tool.

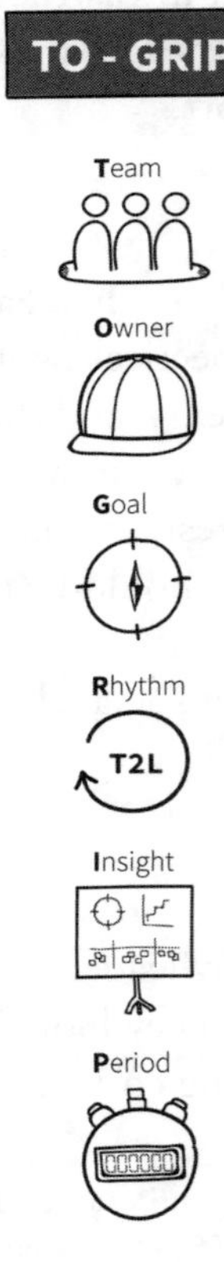

Figure 4.3 Tool 8: TO-GRIP

In a workshop with various employees, TO-GRIP is created and filled in around one theme. Thanks to the six components, the theme becomes very measurable, expectations become explicit, and concrete agreements on the cooperation are made for the coming period.

Let's have a closer look at the parts of this tool.

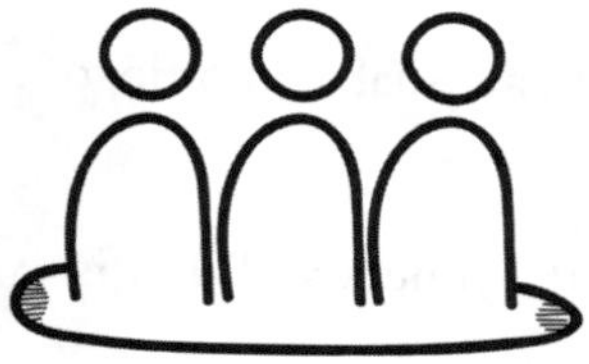

Team

Who will drive the change? Which small team of people will probably have great power in creating the change? This could be an existing team or a newly formed group of people from different teams. This team formally gets the right amount of freedom to take ownership (see Part 2, "Facilitate Ownership"). For example, this mandate could be on setting standards, changing existing rules that block the change, or buying the necessary products.

Owner

Who is the leader behind this change? Who takes responsibility for the consequences or mistakes made during the change? This person is either a manager with a mandate or another person who can quickly get approval on changes needed. This will be the person that drives the change, empowers the team, and sets priorities where needed. He has a (shared) vision for the change on both the current pain and the desired passion (see "How Do You Handle Resistance to Change?" later in this section).

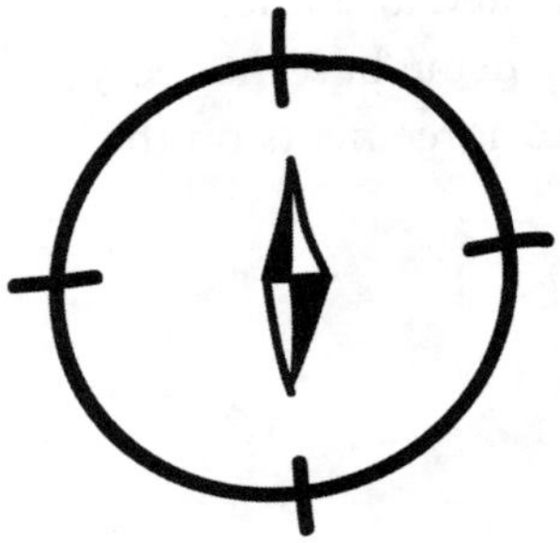

Goal

What is the challenge, problem, or improvement? What is the measurable goal that we want to achieve? How is this translated to a (positive) customer impact? A good practice is to have a tangible metric with a trendline to measure the progress. (See "How Do You Measure Change?" later in this section.)

A good practice is to add a slogan and a visual icon or logo.

Rhythm

When will the team meet? What is the timebox? What is the expected T2L?

In complex environments, the change can't be planned or scheduled. Rhythm is the alternative for a detailed plan. Rhythm builds structure, and it enables us to:

- repeat the inspection of progress and status,
- adapt our approach, and
- inform stakeholders and ask for help.

We don't know yet what we'll be doing after one month, but we do know that every week we'll use the latest insight and experience to improve, and we will keep everybody informed.

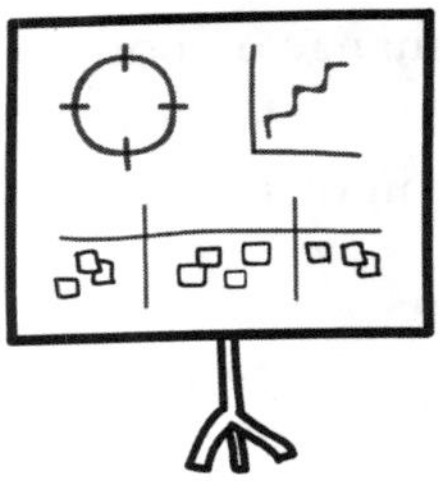

Insight

Insight is a tangible and transparent insight on status and progress. A good practice is to have this on a fixed place physically on the wall. This is where the team members have their rhythm but also where the stakeholders get informed on progress. If somebody else wants to know the status, he can walk to the board and ask for background information. It's based on the concept of visual management.[7]

Tools like VLB, T2L, and KVI are probably used on this insight board.

7. https://www.isixsigma.com/dictionary/visual-controls/

Period

After how many weeks or months do you have a stop-or-continue moment? For which period do we ask for commitment from the team? This is the formal review to see whether we continue. In complex systems, success can't be guaranteed. Sometimes it's better to just stop this improvement and try something totally different. It's a good practice to also celebrate the stop or failure because the organization still learned a lot through trying to improve this particular thing.

The acronym of the six parts results in the name of this tool: TO-GRIP. In this way, both the agile leader and the agile teams have control over improvements, strategic points, or major changes.

Let's have a look at a concrete example of this tool (Table 4.8). A big financial software company already worked with agile for a few years. They are in the midst of implementing a faster way to deploy software by adding automatic tests and automating the deployment of software. But the customers and users are complaining that new functionality takes too long and that when the new functionality is available it doesn't meet the expectations nor does it really work well. Several people want to improve collaboration with real users. They want to use the feedback of the users more intensely. The users who also wanted to collaborate more were called "first users" because they got to see and use the functionality the first. Together with first users, the team members want to launch new functionality and then, when these first users are satisfied with the functionality, it's gradually launched to more customers and users.

Table 4.8 Example of implementing co-creating with users

Team	A few people from different agile teams formed a taskforce to implement this improvement. Most of them got some experience already in working very closely with users. After brainstorming, they gave themselves the name "Co-enablers." They expect that each member will need to spend roughly 4 hours a week to implement the improvements.
Owner	The product manager is the leader behind the change. He really has passion for the topic and can set priorities where needed. He works closely with the development manager who is the hierarchical leader of most of the agile teams.
Goal	During the first meetup of the Co-enablers and the product manager, they brainstormed on a tangible goal. The T2L was quickly picked. Looking at the current implementation of new functionality, they discovered that the T2L currently was between 9 and 15 months. They derived a trendline of the existing T2L. The slogan they created was "Not what I want, but what I need!" described from the perspective of the users.
Rhythm	The team meets every two days. They work on feedback and impediments mentioned by the agile teams. They use the time together mostly to: • Improve the internal wiki with examples, tutorials, and pitfalls. • Share stories of success and failures (to learn from). They prepare the next review meeting with stakeholders. • Formalize changes to be approved by the management team. Every two weeks they have a review meeting[8] lasting an hour. The vision is repeated, stakeholders are updated on the progress made, and larger impediments are shared to find common ground to fix them.
Insight	At a central point, the Co-enablers have posted a large physical board. A good webcam is pointed at it so members of the change group can also meet remotely. They track the progress of several teams in categories of "Waiting," "First steps," "First success," and "Promoter." The 17 agile teams of the department are plotted in these categories to see where they are (see section "How Do You Handle Resistance to Change?" for more details).
Period	The period is set to 9 months. The definition of success is that at least three major new functionalities are successfully done in co-creation with a T2L of less than 1 month, where "successfully done" means an 8 or higher on user satisfaction and more than 25% of the users are using the new functionality.

8. https://www.scrum.org

At www.tval.nl there are several other concrete examples of the use of this tool.

With TO-GRIP, the agile leader can initiate improvements that stimulate an agile culture of collaboration, knowledge sharing, stopping things that don't work, and learning by doing. TO-GRIP offers a concrete tool for more structured solutions. This creates a healthy habit of making major improvements, intervening from the agile leader who contributes to the agile culture. Only then are teams able to continue to grow, cooperate, and take more and more independent initiatives.

How Do You Measure Change?

Is it important to measure the change? Isn't it enough to see the happiness of the people who work on it? Of course the happiness is very important, but always somewhere along the line the question pops up: how are we doing and what did we achieve? Due to micromanaging and measuring the wrong things, some people have an aversion to measuring progress or performance. But when the right things are made transparent and the right ambitions are set, over and over again this brings focus and synergy! It makes the progress transparent and makes explicit what interventions worked and didn't work. Finally, it convinces stakeholders who are still in doubt or even against the change that improvements are made. But how can we measure the change properly?

How can the change be measured in such a way that progress is made transparent? One pitfall is to wait for the final impact of the change on customer satisfaction or even turnover. But often this takes too long to really emerge, and the correlation between the increased happiness and this improvement is at best not one-to-one and is often vague. Another pitfall is to measure only the activity, such as only the number of hours spent on improvements or the number of reports or functionality deployed differently. So how can the change be measured properly?

A practical way to measure is splitting it into three different categories: the output (what is done), the outcome (what is achieved), and the impact (what is the result). Measuring all three gives both focus on the end goal and makes explicit what we have done to reach it. Let's have a look at the co-creation example to explain these three categories (Table 4.9).

Table 4.9 Implementing co-creating with users

Category	Description and Example Metrics
Output	This category measures what has actually already changed and what change has been made. This only measures the activity but not yet the success of the change. For example: • The number of teams that are working with at least one customer in co-creation • The number of teams that deliver to customers at least every month • The number of active participating customers
Outcome	The outcome category measures the first signs of improvements. • The number of customers who are satisfied with the co-creation approach • The average satisfaction of the customers, split into non-participating and participating groupings • The (positive) effect on social media (number of likes, number of forwards, etc.) • The actual reduction of T2L
Impact	The impact category measures what we really want to achieve with the improvement. A combination of impact for the customer and value for the company (see Part 1, "Co-Create Goals," for more information). • The value (turnover) that is received on new or improved products and services • The happiness of the customers and users who are really using it • The number of employees who stayed or even join because of it

How Do You Handle Resistance to Change?

Resistance to change is inevitable and comes in different categories. It's inevitable because teams and individuals in ownership mode (see Part 2) will ask questions and raise their concerns on ideas, practices, or approaches from leaders or other teams. This is often the category of "Let's think it through first," which is a crucial ingredient for their craftsmanship and maturity. Without this natural tendency to resist change, they will go with every new idea and just follow today's wind. The teams ought to resist badly explained change or shallow (not well-thought-out) change. Highly mature teams need a decent critical-thinking hat to start properly with new technologies or new features. Without it, they will overlook the consequences or the long-term effect. The highly mature don't like change, but they love involved improvements. Therefore, most of the resistance is feedback to the agile leader on his behavior. But just as a farmer doesn't blame his crops for not growing or thriving but uses it to adapt and improve his farming skills and create a better environment for his crops, successful agile leaders use the resistance to improve their skills and approaches.

> *Mature teams hate change but love improvements.*

But when resistance is inevitable and has different shapes or categories, how can an agile leader successfully initiate change without being bogged down by resistance? A good way is to know the different categories and have a conversation with the teams about which category they think it is. The latter really drives the crucial culture attributes of transparency and candor. Using tool 8, TO-GRIP, already addresses a lot of the following categories, but still it's good to know and recognize the different shapes of resistance. Let's have a closer look.

The important resistance categories are

- **Why**—Teams need to know the why behind the change. What is the objective, and what is the purpose of it? In co-creation with the informal leaders, this why has to be made explicit so that the change is not really a change but in fact an *improvement*. Again, agile leaders need their teams to resist any badly explained change. This motivates the leader to improve, to stop with bad ideas, and to better explain the improvement and the benefits of it.
- **Urgency**—Tough improvements also need an urgency. If the improvement isn't achieved, something has to (likely) go wrong or tangible opportunities will be missed, such as employees leaving, customers complaining, or new deals being missed. This is especially crucial for tough improvements: they need a lot of effort and investment before the benefits are achieved. This could be in terms of tangible things like fixing bugs or solving long-lasting issues and also intangible things like habits changed or collaboration improved. Often this resistance is not explicit. People and teams like the improvement but, after a few weeks, nothing has really changed. When

asked, people like to improve and spent time on it, but again in hindsight no real investment was made. Therefore, this resistance is not on the individual level nor on the team level, but on the system level (see Peter Senge and his work on system thinking[9]). Often, both setting clear priorities and supporting the teams to really spend time on it are crucial to conquering this resistance on the system level.

- **How**—Depending on the maturity of the team, the how should be clear. Teams at a low maturity level need more details than highly mature teams (see Part 2 for more details). This resistance on the how comes in different shapes. People can resist instructions or approaches. To the leader, it may seem that they resist the whole, but actually they only resist several parts. Others can resist change because the unknown frightens them. Giving more details on how the change will look and what the consequences are often removes this fear of the unknown. In communicating with different teams, successful leaders incorporate both in their stories. They find the balance in giving details and examples without prescribing it to the more mature teams. It's often better when several informal leaders give examples regarding how the change will look.
- **Forced**—This is one of the most difficult categories. These people and teams are resistant to the improvement because they feel they are forced into it. They might see the benefit, the urgency, and the how, but they just don't want to change because it's mandatory. It's one of the most difficult categories because the resistance could be based on egos or because they don't get enough freedom based on their maturity. For an agile leader to know which of the two it is is difficult because the perceived behavior of the people and the team are the same. Informal leaders showing resistance because of their egos is bad. The agile leader should often be very strict and sometimes even be harsh to these informal leaders. Their egos should never be more important than the benefit and well-being of the whole. But when the agile leader makes a wrong judgment and is harsh toward the well-intentioned informal leader, it's likely that transparency, trust, and openness go down the drain. Also, when the agile leader isn't harsh and doesn't publicly criticize the attitude of the informal leader, the culture of group-interest, sharing, and helping is going down the same drain. Trying

9. https://www.amazon.com/Fifth-Discipline-Practice-Learning-Organization-ebook/dp/B000SEIFKK

to really understand the informal leader and have a heart-to-heart conversation before making decisions is a practical tip.

- **Change fatigue**—The last two categories are feedback that is particular to the agile leader's attitude and communication. Teams and people that show this type of resistance are often still working to harvest the fruit of the previous improvements and don't want to work on another improvement just yet. They know the why, the how, and also the urgency. But other improvements are still going on. Successful agile leaders don't start a lot of individual improvements; rather, they tell the journey and the dot on the horizon and let teams and individuals decide on the speed and ordering of the improvements needed to reach the dot. They overcommunicate the overarching story and objectives and are *experimentors* of the learning journey.
- **Fear**—Being afraid of the unknown is a natural emotion. When the department is scared about the upcoming change, it's often because they doubt the effect it will have on them. The fear can be for their job security, of being unable to achieve the change, of having insufficient skills, of being unsuccessful in their new role, or of working together with people they don't know or just don't like. All kinds of fear could be present but are often because they don't trust the leader to make the change successful, or they may doubt the motivations of the agile leader behind the change. A leader of a financial organization overcame the fear within his department by just being radically open about the things he didn't know yet and the things he didn't like about the necessary change. But he showed confidence that together they will make the change successful. And both his history and his latest results proved that he was very well able to lead an organization through fears of the unknown.

A practical way to solve resistance is, first of all, to accept that resistance to change is crucial because this will also result in a steady status afterward. When the people see the value in the new way of working, they will start to lower resistance and start being an enabler for change. They will voluntarily take ownership of the ambition and make the change successful. They will show the same resistance again when a change is proposed that wants to throw away the successful change.

It's the role of the agile leader to use the power of the change team and to give them enough structure so they can enable the change in the rest of the organization. The practical tool TO-GRIP will support the agile leader in this structure by showing confidence and giving enough mandate and authority to this change team together with a tangible goal, powerful rhythm, transparent insight, and clear evaluation moment. These ingredients of the TO-GRIP tool will help the agile leader to create a successful and powerful culture for continuous learning and improvement.

Summary of Part 4—Design Healthy Habits

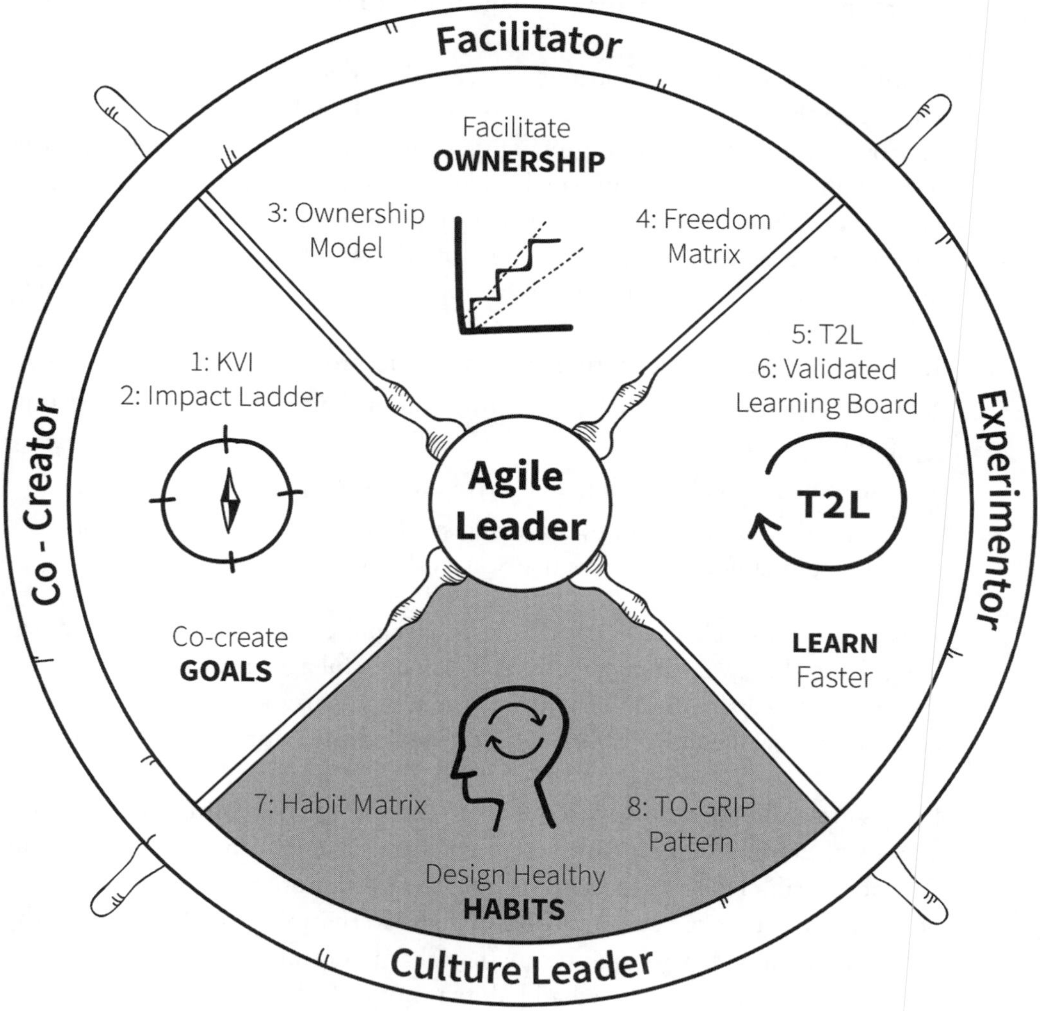

Agile leaders give their teams a lot of freedom, space, trust, and inspiration for their daily work to increase their customer impact. They shift to the background and do not feel the need to be needed nor to interfere with the daily work. If the goals are inspiring (Part 1), if the teams take ownership (Part 2), and if the T2L is short (Part 3), the agile leader can focus on the culture. He can repair and improve this and thus create an increasingly better environment for his self-managing agile teams to thrive.

Culture follows structure (Larman's law) and therefore continuously improving things like KVI, the Ownership Model, and the T2L is crucial for improving the culture. But improving the culture also requires designing better habits and influencing the informal leaders. See the previous figure for an overview of the tools in Part 4 that will support the agile leader in improving the culture. Besides continuously improving the structure, the underlying habits and informal influencers can be improved by following these four steps:

1. Discover a part of the culture you want to improve.
2. Together with a few people, brainstorm on the habits that drive the existing culture.
3. Discover new, healthy habits that drive the desired improvement.
4. Anchor the improvement by adjusting symbols (reports, overviews, lists) and guiding informal leaders (heroes) to show the right behavior.

This drives culture change by continuously changing small parts—not with a big-bang change but by creating a viral change. Successful agile leaders have a keen eye for both the habits and the influencers in the organization because they understand how these two can be used to continuously improve the environment.

Habits are an important way to influence and change the culture. Habits are actions of employees and teams, triggered by a situation, that are rewarded in the short term. This makes the behavior more and more routine. Habits can be used to improve the culture by finding an alternative for bad and unhealthy habits. Bad habits have a long-term effect that undermine the desired agile culture. The solution to these bad habits is not to forbid them or enforce a changed behavior but to reward new behavior in the short term. As a result, the negative long-term effect of bad habits is replaced by the positive long-term effect of new good habits. This creates a better culture. The Habit Matrix helps to recognize unhealthy habits and replace them with healthy habits. This seventh tool for agile leaders clarifies habits, triggers, or cues; the short-term incentive; and the long-term consequences. With the Habit

Matrix, brainstorming can be done to discover new habits that do contribute to the agile culture.

As habits continue to improve, it is important that the agile leader focuses on symbols and heroes. The heroes are the informal influencers of the teams. The symbols are reports, overviews, and bonuses. By connecting symbols and heroes to the desired agile culture, the new culture is actually anchored.

Finally, it is important that improvements and strategic themes involving multiple teams are also part of the agile culture. TO-GRIP, a set of six components, helps the agile leader to implement improvements and strategic themes in a constructive manner. With this eighth tool from the toolkit, the agile leader stimulates the culture of teamwork between teams, improving the customer's impact and quickly learning from feedback from users.

The Agile Leader as Culture Leader

If the going is tough, if pressure is on, it is all the more important that the agile leader guards the culture. Because if, under pressure, short-term incentives of good behavior are not met, it will destroy collaboration, long-term investment, and mutual learning. This is automatically the moment when unhealthy habits can quickly take root. The carefully constructed and costly agile culture can crumble. Agile leaders recognize these moments and then come to the stage. They stick out their necks, show guts, pull teams through the difficult period, and continue to restore and improve the culture. That makes them real leaders.

Concrete Questions

The following are some questions to put the tools, examples, and ideas from Part 4 into practice.

1. In which situations is it especially difficult for you to be a leader?
2. What habits do you create for yourself to stay healthy as a leader?
3. Who will inspire you and motivate you? And who will serve as motivation when you go through a tough time?

Notes

After Reading This Book

Now that you've read this book, let's revisit the main theme and the reasons why we needed a new toolkit. This will support you in implementing the tools and effectively developing the mindset needed.

WHY A NEW TOOLKIT?

The world around us is changing faster and faster. As Kotter says, "The greatest challenge business leaders face today is how to stay competitive amid constant turbulence and disruption."[1] New technologies, new market opportunities, and new competitors emerge unexpectedly and unpredictably. This is why agile and working with agile teams is becoming more and more popular. This requires a new way of leading organizations. Agile leaders lead their teams in this completely new way. They lead because they create precisely the environment that their self-managing teams need in order to grow and thrive. Within this environment, the teams optimize the processes themselves, increase their own effectiveness and efficiency, and make all kinds of decisions on a daily basis. That makes these teams self-managing. They organize their own work and have all the skills to do that. These agile teams are agile in and of themselves, because they can respond quickly to new technologies, threats from competitors, and the ever-changing expectations of their customers. They don't have to wait for official approval, management decisions, or top-down strategic changes. Because they have a short feedback loop with their customers and users, they can continuously experiment with new ideas, improve their products and services, and align with other self-managing teams.

The agile leader is the architect of this environment. He takes the humble responsibility to create this environment for his people and teams. When the teams don't flourish, when things go wrong, or when customers are not satisfied, the new leader doesn't punish his people for doing wrong things. Instead, he sees it as feedback of the environment he created. He asks for help from his employees to find improvement, and together they adapt and improve the environment.

1. https://hbr.org/2012/11/accelerate

Agile Leadership Toolkit

Agile leaders provide an inspiring environment for their agile teams to thrive. But how do they create such an engaging environment? This requires not only a new mindset but a lot of new skills. They must unlearn the old skills and learn the new ones. They become masters in leading inspiring environments because they practice a lot—just as a chef doesn't become a chef by reading a book but by preparing thousands of meals with tools ranging from knives to ovens. To help agile leaders, this book provides practical tools, metrics, and examples that are put immediately into practice and grow along the journey. Learn by doing.

Where to Start

The tools described in this book are split into four components (Figure 5.1). As mentioned at the start of this book, the tools can be used independently

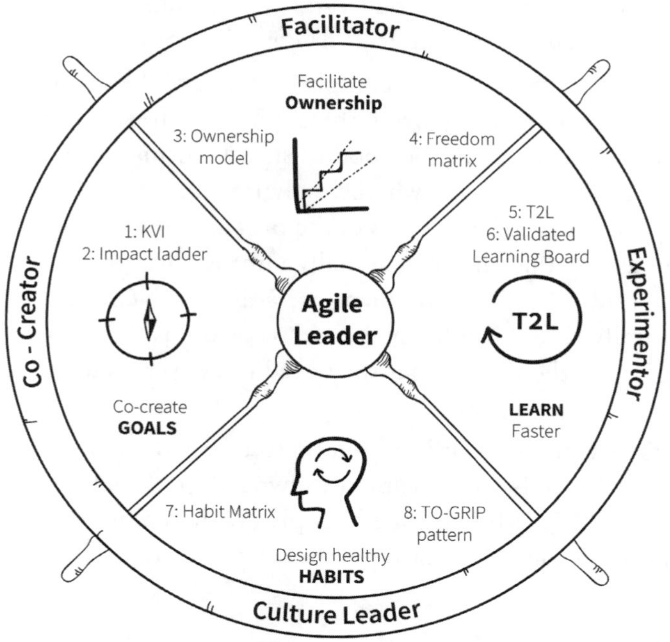

Figure 5.1 The four tool components

and don't have a strict order. To explain the tools in this book, I used the top-down approach. Starting with goals, working down to ownership, learning from customers, and, last but not least, working continuously on the culture.

Several managers who started to use the tools somehow started with the Ownership Model (Tool 3). Others started with the T2L metric (Tool 5). I often advise a starting place that's based on the immediate pain or frustration within the organization. Let's have a closer look at common pains and determine the most practical tools to start with.

- **Demotivated teams.** If teams are passive, people are leaving, or the managers feel that they constantly have to push the teams to do more, it's probably good to begin with the Ownership Model (Tool 5) and the Freedom Matrix (Tool 4). Also, have a candid workshop with several representatives of the teams on what ownership is and what kills it.
- **Lack of focus.** If too many things are important, or if priorities switch constantly, it's probably good to start by introducing a KVI (Tool 1) with a focus on the customer and what drives value for the organization.
- **Low quality.** Are customers complaining about the quality of the product or service? Are teams ignoring these quality issues or don't know how to solve them? If so, it may be good to start by using the Validated Learning Board (Tool 6) and track whether solving bugs are also reducing complaints. This often fosters in the organization the belief that they can fix things and that they can actually improve the quality. Next, it gives a little confidence to your frequent users that problems are actually being structurally solved. Probably a good next tool is the Ownership Model (Tool 5); ask the teams what they need to deliver quality and actually be proud of what they create.
- **Talents leaving.** Is it hard to hold on to talented people or recruit talented people? Two tools could help out: Ownership Model (Tool 3) and Habit Matrix (Tool 7). Most talented people are driven by the autonomy[2] they are given to grow their mastery and craftsmanship. The Ownership Model

2. Daniel Pink, "The surprising truth about what motivates people." https://www.youtube.com/watch?v=u6XAPnuFjJc

shows that people leave when the have too much *and* too little autonomy. The Habit Matrix can be used to drive the learning culture.

- **Lack of customer focus.** If employees focus on their own work and don't keep the customer in mind, a good tool to start with is the T2L metric (Tool 5). Reducing the customer-learning delay in the organization is crucial to having customer focus. When it takes months for employees to get feedback on their work from the customer's perspective, having a customer focus is hardly possible. Starting with a workshop to visualize the current T2L and brainstorm ways to minimize it is an insightful and energizing way to begin. Using that feedback and TO-GRIP pattern (Tool 8) is a practical step forward.

Complex Environment

The environment that the agile teams need is complex. It's never been done before for this specific group of people, and what's needed for success can't be analyzed upfront or copied from other organizations. It's the unique environment that the teams need at this moment in time. After a while, the environment needed can be different due to all kinds of reasons, like a change in the people who work at the company, growth of teams, new technologies, and new market situations. Continuous improvement of the environment and especially the underlying culture needs the constant focus of the agile leader—not because he's so smart and can oversee everything, but because he uses the collective insight of different people. Not because he builds on previous successes, but because he asks for help openly and candidly.

Structure and Culture

By both improving the structure (tangible things like meetings, metrics, mandates, and overviews) and improving the culture (intangible things like habits and heroes), the agile leader can continuously improve the environment. If, for example, he wants to improve the customer-centric nature of the culture, improving the T2L is often a good first step because it gives teams quick feedback from actual users. Having a tangible KVI supports the customer focus. But also, having a keen eye for habits and heroes is crucial to anchor a customer-centric culture.

The tools in this book support the agile leader in continuously improving the environment, both for the tangible as well as the intangible.

SKETCH, GO, LEARN

The implementation of every tool in this toolkit is complex. It can't be analyzed upfront what the tool should look like. Sketching a first version of the tool, experiencing how the tool works in real life, and learning along the way are the only ways to implement a good version of each tool. Getting honest feedback on how the tool really works on the "floor" is crucial to improving the environment. This requires the agile leader to be candid and vulnerable toward his agile teams while implementing the different tools. The leader has to be vulnerable, admitting that he doesn't own the truth or have all the answers, and candid, showing his passion and drive to continuously improve and asking others to be honest as well and to verbalize what they think and feel.

The eighth tool, TO-GRIP, can be used for many things, from improving marketing campaigns to improving the quality of products. This can also be said for implementing any of the other tools in the book. Creating a group of people to support and drive the change will help the agile leader. Asking a few people to give honest feedback on how the change really is going and to brainstorm together on improvements with a steady rhythm is a powerful way to continuously improve the environment, one step at the time.

FIND PEERS

At different locations throughout the world, we want to create a local community of peers who work with these tools. Contact me through the website www.tval.nl to start or join a local community. I want to create a community where agile leaders learn from each other and share discoveries, mistakes, challenges, and successes.

Have fun with your own journey in becoming a better agile leader for your self-managing teams so they can thrive!

Index

Pearson
livelessons™
Photo by marvent/Shutterstock

Photo by izusek/gettyimages